How to Journal for Hope and Happiness:

Journey to the Christian Heart in 5 simple steps

Diane C. Doyle

How to Journal for Hope and Happiness:
Journey to the Christian Heart in 5 simple steps

ISBN 10: 1-933817-66-6
ISBN 13: 978-1-933817-66-8

Published by: Profits Publishing
http://profitspublishing.com

Canadian Address
1265 Charter Hill Drive
Coquitlam, BC, V3E 1P1
Phone: (604) 941-3041
Fax: (604) 944-7993

US Address
1300 Boblett Street
Unit A-218
Blaine, WA 98230
Phone: (866) 492-6623
Fax: (250) 493-6603

What Others Say About This Book

"Journaling is such a wonderful tool for spiritual growth and for acquiring deeper self knowledge that aids in building character. Sketchajournal is a great practical and insightful resource that will fuel the fire of faith in dry times and take you to new levels of contemplative prayer. Get ready to soar to new heights with the help of this book! Diane's examples, analogies and step by step program will help you intellectually grasp the concepts of prayer so that your heart can explore the depth of prayer's purpose and transforming power."

Janelle Reinhart
Christian Singer, Songwriter
www.janelle.cc

Some of the important keys to my success in publishing have been prayer and journaling. I believe it is the "missing link" when it comes to Success. Too many entrepreneurs forget or overlook this powerful process. Diane's book is jammed packed with nuggets you can use to increase your spiritual well being and on the way drive up your wealth 10 fold. Do not wait another minute pick up this book and live the life you deserve!

Jeff McCallum
Author of the # 1 Amazon Best Seller
101 Reasons Why You Must Write A Book:
How To Make A Six Figure Income
By Writing & Publishing Your Own Book

"WOW, great idea Diane. I often draw pictures, charts and mind maps in my journal. Pictures bring our relationships and interconnections better than words. As I create conceptual pictures my journaling is much easier as I interpret ideas and add more meat to new insights. Allowing these 2 processes on opposite pages grounds my creativity. I already started doing this in my journal and enjoy my creative big picture journey sketches and my written details more each day. Keep up the great work."

John Robson
www.Higher Awareness.com
www.journalingtools.com
Edmonton, Alberta

"Journaling will open new avenues to emotional spiritual and health benefits. Personally as a retired nurse I found it very beneficial to help me cope with the feelings of uselessness that came with retirement after a busy lifestyle. By taking time to put on paper your emotional feelings of frustrations, joy, rejection and love, it will clarify your priorities and diminish the negative feelings you may have towards yourself or others. It opens the door to the spiritual part of our lives which is often neglected when we are too busy. Journaling helped me find the joy, peace and contentment necessary to put my priorities in the right place."

Juliette Jones
Retired Nurse
St. Antoine de Tilly, Quebec

"I think Diane has developed a very interesting and unique concept. Her writing style is engaging, creative, enthusiastic and inspiring. The five-step program included in this book is a very powerful tool to help everyone reach balance in their life and to find peace of mind and above all, happiness."

Celeste Lozano
Entrepreneur and Mentor
Gibsons, British Columbia

"Journaling in combination with sketching is the fastest way I know of to start really manifesting what you truly want in life. The tools in this book are life changing and anyone can use them."

Bob Burnham Author of the # 1 Amazon Best Seller:
101 Reasons Why You Must Write A Book:
How To Make A Six Figure Income
By Writing & Publishing Your Own Book

"As an educator, I have seen the power of deeper self-awareness to bring about dramatic and lasting change. "How to Journal for Hope and Happiness" is a wonderful companion and learning tool for anyone embarking on the journey of discovering the amazing person each of us are created and called to be. Ms. Doyle succeeds in succinctly explaining the process, and making it fun at the same time!"

Heidi Vanstone
Educator
Waterloo, Ontario

"I would highly recommend Diane Doyle's book on journaling. Her book sets out five easy to follow steps that will draw you into a closer relationship with God. Do you long to hear God's voice? Simple creative journaling is a powerful tool to help you to hear from God, and allow Him to guide you through life's journey."

Cecilia Kozak
Mustard Prayer Group
Burnaby, British Columbia

5-Step Workshop Participants

"It was very inspiring and totally engaging. A fascinating process."

Karen Shibley-Fry
Gracepoint Community Church

"It helped me to work through some very tough emotional issues with work and to be able to acknowledge it and let it go and forgive through writing out words, then putting pictures to it and finding scripture to solidify and heal."

Janice Doerksen R.H.N.
Friends Langley Vineyard

> **"I never know what I think about something until I've read what I've written."**
> **William Faulkner**

Dedication

I want to thank my amazing husband for all his support and encouragement. First, I thank him for the support to take a year leave from my employment to venture into my entrepreneurial dreams. Second , I thank him for the encouragement to write this book and by promoting the SketchaJournal business to the people he comes in contact with. I want to thank my step-daughter Emma for welcoming me into her life at the young age of 7 and making me feel accepted and loved from the very beginning. I also thank Amber May, who had a very short time with us but has left a great impact on our lives, as well as junior, who reminds me of surprises and miracles. My love and my appreciation go to my parents, siblings, and extended family and friends for their experiences and support throughout my journey. My appreciation also goes to the many writers, workshop and retreat leaders, mentors, and teachers that have all shared ideas that have made me who I am today.

Thanks to:

The Association of Neighbourhood Houses of British Columbia for having employee policies that are flexible, and my Executive Director Karen Larcombe in granting a year leave from my position as Team Leader at South Vancouver Neighbourhood House.

Everyone who took the time to read the manuscript and who offered comments and testimonials.

I want to thank Karen Shibley-Fry for transforming my pencil sketches and ideas into graphic design for the original SketchaJournal logo and notebooks and Don Edlund for the book cover.

Claudette Carracedo from Claudette Carracedo Photo for her professionalism in photography and the picture on the back cover.

Profits Publishing and Rebecca Hanna for making a manuscript into a tangible book.

I thank, with gratitude, my Wonderful Creator, the Good Lord, and the movement of the Holy Spirit, who have journeyed with me through the good, the bad, and the ugly. Thank you for being my spiritual companion and hope.

Forward

It is an honour and a privilege to be asked to write this forward. During the more than twenty years that I have personally known Diane, I have been afforded the rare gift of seeing her growth and transitions through her life experiences; I have viewed both her joy and her pain. Through it all, Diane has become a faith-filled woman who is gifted in helping others grow closer to their God. Seeing her use this gift and make her mission in this life even more alive by launching a business and writing a book is truly inspiring!

It has been a special treat to be able to read some of the rough drafts of this book and to see it grow and develop into what I must say is a work of art (no pun intended) rather than just a literary endeavour. One of the things that I like best in Diane's book is the way that she takes a potentially very complex topic and makes it sound so simple. She is able to take concepts from the worlds of journaling, sketching, scripture, personal growth, and psychobiology to develop a program that will enrich your day-to-day life by enriching your spiritual life. That she is able to present this in a simple and very user-friendly format that stays away from any jargon is a feat to be admired.

But just reading the book would miss so much of what the book has to offer. I love the sketches! They bring life to the book and help to explain concepts that can be difficult to grasp just through the written word. It is amazing how simple, rudimentary sketches can be deeply moving or can give you a light and airy feeling of freedom and joy. Incorporating sketching into journaling reminds me of some of the most significant times in my life. Although I would often journal when struggling with issues, when I recall the most critical or difficult times in my life, I remember drawing as well. I can now understand why this was so essential while working through the important moments of my life. So, it only makes sense to add sketching to an area as important as your spiritual life.

What is encouraging in Diane's book is that she is able to present a process to transform your life that is simple and straightforward, but also adaptable to so many situations. I think of the work that I do with those struggling with mental health issues and addictions and can think of many times where SketchaJournaling would help clients in ways that talk therapy never could. The process is not intimidating and allows you to delve into some of the complex, or hidden, parts of your life in a very gentle way. It can be as simple or as complex as a person chooses to make it. It can be done in very short blocks of time or at a leisurely pace. A person can choose to focus on the different aspects of the book. For the person who likes the written word, they can read the book; those who enjoy the visual or creative side can appreciate the sketches; those focused on scripture can read and ponder scripture; or one can bring it all together and work at the exercises involved in SketchaJournaling. Whichever way you choose, I am sure that you will not put the book down without getting something out of it.

So I invite you to begin your journey. I wish you well on your spiritual path. I know that you have a wonderful guide, and I trust that SketchaJournaling will help you to transform your life.

Denise Nedelec, MSW

Table of Contents

Introduction

God your Creator wants to speak to you_____(insert name) personally, like no other person in the world. God uses scripture, friends, family, your history, and experiences. He also uses your thoughts, views, positive moments, and the challenges of life. God is calling you today, in this very moment, to be authentic and whole: to live a life full of hope.

"'For I know the plans that I have for you,' declares the LORD, 'plans for welfare and not for calamity to give you a future and a hope.'"
Jeremiah 29:11

Are you ready for a personal experience? Use your thoughts, reflections, and creativity to be actively contemplative in your journey towards abundant life. Use this 5-Step SketchaJournal Program to personalize scripture on your heart and in your life. With scripture as a foundation, find out what God is really saying to you_____(insert name).

You will learn how to

- Personalize your experience of scripture
- Sketch out the images that come to your mind
- Sit and absorb the Word
- Act and live the Word
- You will find out when, where, what, why, and how scripture relates to you
- You will learn what scripture means to you at this present moment
- You will gain HOPE and FREEDOM that will last a lifetime

How This Book is Organized

There are several helpful features that you will find in this book. First of all, the book is divided into two main Sections. The first Section describes all the benefits of journaling and why you must Journal to bring hope and happiness into your life.

The second Section breaks down the 5-Step SketchaJournal (SJ) Program so that it is easy to understand and follow. It has a clear description, examples, and exercises that will lead you through the steps. The steps are simple steps but that is not to be confused with easy steps. I say it may not be easy because at some point you may need to shift your thought process or make changes in your life that might require a commitment or strong resolve to make the changes. The Holy Spirit, your advocate, will be with you through it all and will encourage you to lead a life worthy of your calling. The Holy Spirit will also lead you in celebration, which is an important part of the 5-Step SJ Program. You will find in the margins of most pages a scripture passage and a small sketch that depicts the message of the page. In **Section 2** you will find the 5 steps listed on the bottom of each page for easy reference.

You will find icons so that you can quickly find examples 👀 , exercises 🐝 , and personal notes ⟨Personal Note⟩ throughout the book.

The Bible verses are from MSG, ASV, NASB, NLT, and WE. I encourage you to cross reference with your own Bible as each translation will give you a slightly different feel of the scripture.

Stick-people sketches are used for quick visuals that are easy to draw and easy to understand. The simplicity of the sketch will help you to focus on the meaning and message of the page and can be quickly referred to by flipping through the pages.

Definitions are used to explain a number of words, and additional scriptures, references, and quotes are used throughout the book. The book makes use of visual creative tools that use the right brain (your emotions, visual, and creative side) as well, there are many ideas that make use of the left brain (your logical, linear, and detailed side).

Discover and remember the unique features of the left and right functions of your brain by the simplified sketch below.

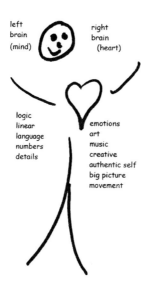

left
brain
(mind)

right
brain
(heart)

logic
linear
language
numbers
details

emotions
art
music
creative
authentic self
big picture
movement

Intro to the 5-Step SketchaJournal (SJ) Program

"I came that they may have life, and have it abundantly."
John 10:10b

"But you will receive power when the Holy Spirit comes upon you. And you will be my witnesses, telling people about me everywhere— in Jerusalem, throughout Judea, in Samaria, and to the ends of the earth."
Acts 1:8

You will be inspired by the 5-Step SJ Program. It is a technique that will bring hope and adventure to your Christian Journey. It will provide a starting point in your current life and will transform your journey so that you can have a future full of hope and abundance.

The framework of the 5-Step SJ Program is to use journaling and sketching tools that will help you to go deeper in your relationship with God and grow in your relationships with people.

People have gained confidence, insight, motivation, and renewed hope through the process of the 5-Step SJ Program.

You too will experience these benefits and more, as you learn each step and practice it in your life.

The 5 simple steps to revitalizing your prayer life are to :

1. **Meditate**: What word is surfacing for you right now?
2. **Contemplate**: What does this mean? Sit with it and ponder. Find relevant scripture.
3. **Activate**: Sketch the image of the scripture, and journal using your heart and mind to discover a message of hope and happiness in your life.
4. **Liberate**: Decide what your next step will be and act on it.

5. **Celebrate**: Thank God for inspiring your personal journey, and commit to an activity that renews you.

In **Section 2** you will learn the details of each step, read examples, and practice activities to solidify each concept.

Each step makes use of journaling tools to help you focus on how God is working in your life today.

> Personal Note

I have been journaling since I was eight years old. The concept of journaling is not new to me. As an adult, I became interested in prayer and meditation, later incorporating pictures into my prayer journal. By drawing, I was able to gain new perspectives and gain insights to my prayer time. More recently I took it a step further: learning about the right and left brain and discovering how sketching and journaling together can bring hope and happiness.

In the 5-Step SJ Program you will notice I take the concept of balancing the right and left brain (or heart and mind) and incorporate contemplation and activation. My goal is to help you to bring balance in your life by using scripture for encouragement, moving it to action, and living your authentic self. Before launching the program I tested the 5 steps in a number of different areas in my life, and I was always surprised that they worked. You too will be surprised regardless of the vastness of your concerns. There will always be a message for you, be it about business, work, relationships, personal matters, goal setting, faith journey, or emotional matters. You will discover a message each time you move through the 5 steps. As you use the tools, God will reveal some lessons.

"Make me know Your ways, O LORD; Teach me Your paths. Lead me in Your truth and teach me."
Psalm 25:4-5a

What is a SketchaJournal™ (SJ)?

You will see a sample of a SketchaJournal (SJ) page in **Appendix B**. A SketchaJournal is used to help facilitate the process of the 5 - Step SJ Program. A SketchaJournal is two books merged into one. It is similar to a sketch book where you can be creative in using your right brain on blank pages. You also have the use of lined pages to Journal, which makes use of your left-brain function. You are welcome to photocopy the template to facilitate the 5 steps or purchase a SketchaJournal for the Christian Heart that is already printed and bound at www.SketchaJournal.com.

Section 1 of this book uses scripture and examples to explain the 21 benefits of SJ journaling in your prayer time. It is important for you to embrace the benefits of journaling so you can incorporate it easily in your prayer life and each day. The more you can relate to the benefits the easier it will be to develop the practice of journaling as a positive tool that will infuse your life with HOPE and HAPPINESS!

Enjoy this new adventure that is waiting to unfold in your life.

Section 1

Then our mouth was filled with laughter
And our tongue with joyful shouting;
Then they said among the nations,
The LORD has done great things for them.
The LORD has done great things for us;
We are glad.
Psalm 126:2-3

The LORD bless you, and keep you;
The LORD make His face shine on you,
And be gracious to you;
The LORD lift up His countenance on you,
And give you peace.
Numbers 6:24-26

Chapter 1

21 Reasons Why You Must Journal for Hope and Happiness

Reason 1

Discover How the Best Way to Find Harmony is Through Contemplation and Action

"Be still, and know that I am God."
Psalm 46:10a

"Be doers of the Word...a doer who acts such a one shall be blessed in what they do."
James 1:22,25b

Figure 1
Contemplative Action

The beauty of the 5-Step SJ Program is that it seeks to be actively contemplative. Time is spent in each step being both reflective and active.

Steps 1 and 2 provide the foundation to identify your current journey in the present moment. Scripture is identified as a starting point for your prayer time. Step 3 focuses on sketching and journaling to balance your right and left brain thinking. Steps 4 and 5 will motivate you in decision - making, action, and celebration.

To renew ourselves we must have both quiet and active moments. The journey will be different if you are an introvert or an extrovert. By being attentive and aware of what renews you, you can decide if you need more quiet time or more interaction with people. Journaling will help you to identify if you are balanced in your quiet and active activities.

Growing up in the prairies, the four seasons were very distinct. Winters were cold and snowy, summers were very hot and sunny, spring meant new life, and fall meant harvest time. I recently bought a hologram

of a large tree in a field with distant trees and fields surrounding the focal tree. As you look at the image at different angles you see the tree in different seasons; spring, summer, winter, and fall. At certain angles you even see a mix of seasons where it blends the two seasons or you can see the start of a season changing to another.

"For everything there is a season, a time for every activity under heaven.
A time to be born and a time to die.
A time to plant and a time to harvest."
Ecclesiastes 3:1-2

In looking at nature and creation they reveal that there is a time for hibernation/quiet, a time for growth, and a time to reproduce or bear fruit. With today's fast-paced world we can be active twenty-four hours a day.

When is your chance to be contemplative? Journaling is a must to experience contemplation in your life.

Reason 2

Experience How Scripture Can Truly Change Your Life

**Figure 2
Journaling
Brings Scripture
Alive**

Journaling brings scripture alive for you. Scripture will become relevant to your life as you are living it today.

That is why it is called the living word. You might read the Bible like a historical document to help you understand past people and events. This makes it difficult for a person to make the jump from historical to the living word.

A helpful tip to bring scripture alive is by reading a scripture passage and inserting your own name in the appropriate places. To take it one step further, you can write down the scripture with your name and then read it aloud. By writing and hearing yourself speak, you are engaging the left and right sides of the brain, which will strengthen the personalized message for you. You are using visual, audible, and tactile senses, which maximize your experience and ownership of the scripture.

Example 1

Numbers 7:24-27

The Lord bless you and keep you

The Lord let his face shine upon you and

Be generous to you!

The Lord look upon you kindly and give you peace!

(Notes: Let his face shine: a Hebrew idiom for "smile." Peace: the Hebrew word includes the idea of "prosperity, happiness.")

Personalized

Lord Bless me Diane Doyle and keep me safe, hold me, be with me! Lord shine your face on me Diane and my family and friends.

Example 2

Acts 1:8

But you will receive power when the Holy Spirit comes upon you, and you will be my witnesses in Jerusalem, throughout Judea and Samaria and to the ends of the earth.

Personalized

I Diane will receive confidence, courage, and reassurance when the Holy Spirit touches my heart and mind, and I will share my story to my friends, family, and work place here in Vancouver, B.C. and wherever life takes me.

 Exercise

Can you feel the difference when scripture comes alive for you? Is God speaking to your heart and mind right now? The more you read and write down scripture and add images, the more you will identify with the lesson and incorporate it in your life. Spend some time right now to try this exercise.

How would you personalize these two scriptures?

Exercise 1

Numbers 7:24–27

The Lord bless you and keep you. The Lord let his face shine upon you and be generous to you!

_____
_____
_____
_____
_____
_____
_____
_____
_____
_____

Exercise 2

Acts 1:8

But you will receive power when the Holy Spirit comes upon you. And you will be my witnesses, telling people about me everywhere—in Jerusalem, throughout Judea, in Samaria, and to the ends of the earth.

_____

_____

_____

_____

_____

_____

_____

_____

_____

_____

_____

Reason 3

Discover the Authentic You that God Created You to Be

"He raiseth up the poor out of the dust, He lifteth up the needy from the dunghill, To make them sit with princes, And inherit the throne of glory: For the pillars of the earth are Jehovah's, And he hath set the world upon them."
1 Samuel 2:8

"The LORD will withhold no good thing from those who do what is right. Yes, ask me for anything in my name, and I will do it!"
Psalm 84:11b

Have you ever been uncomfortable in your own skin? I have, and it's not a pleasant feeling. You know, when everything seems awkward and challenging and you have butterflies in your stomach and your heart is racing. Now remember a time when you were completely content and felt "this is good"—everything feels right at this very moment. That is what people want: to feel true to their gifts, talents, and interests. That is what you and I want. We all want to grow and be challenged in a way that is authentic, and there will growing pains with that. But where is the core or tiny seed that is your true self and how do you make sure it is protected and nourished?

When I was in grade 10 we had to take typing in school. I wasn't good at it and I wasn't motivated, nor did I put value to it. At the time, typing to me meant being a secretary. This was before computers made such a huge impact on society. Later in University, I would pay people to type my hand-written papers for me. For seven years I was working in an office and had to deal with writing grants, emails, and correspondence.

My frustration grew as I didn't like sitting at a desk, but this is where I found myself.

I felt inadequate and stuck in a downward spiral. Typing was just a small portion of my job but it pulled the energy out of me. My self confidence was being challenged. Today I am hand writing this book and I feel energized; I feel creative and I feel authentic to my true personality. Yes, I'm also typing it, and it is still painful but that is after my creative draft is finished.

"The Kingdom of Heaven is like a treasure that a man discovered hidden in a field. In his excitement, he hid it again and sold everything he owned to get enough money to buy the field." Matthew 13:44

To find your true authenticity is exhilarating and liberating. Journaling will assist you in becoming the authentic person that God has created you to be. You cannot deny the words that you yourself have written in your own handwriting in your own personal journal. If you happen to write something that is not authentic or true you will have a small nagging voice in your head saying, "This isn't true … what are you saying?" Of course some people will try to start their journal so they look like a better person, but there are several journaling tools that will help you unwrap what is not your authentic self so over time you will be quicker to identify for yourself what is your true being and what is your false self. No more facades or pretending. You will be relaxed, calm, at peace, and receptive to the lessons in life.

**Figure 3
Authentic Me
God created
me**

On the other hand, some people start with a negative self-image and feel their self-worth is not valuable. By taking quiet time, slowing down your thoughts, and taking time alone, you will slowly understand your value in God's relationship and with the people in your community. Journaling will force you to be true to yourself and when you strip away all the negative thoughts and feelings about yourself you will find the pearl of great price.

This reminds me of a cute joke where a little boy was shovelling manure from a huge pile. When asked why he would 'take time' to shovel manure he replied quickly and positively. "You can't fool me. If there is all this horse manure here, there has to be a horse hiding here somewhere."

We too might have a lot of dung clinging to us but there is a beautiful spirit inside of you. Journaling will help you to find your authentic spirit.

Reason 4

Banish Regrets and Live Guilt-FREE

I believe true carefree happiness means you will look back on your life and say, "I made the best choices possible." As a Christian you can make these decisions with your Creator and feel good because you made your choices based on God's standard of love and respect. I find it heart-rending when people are still living with regrets in their lives. It is not only the older population at the end of their lives, it is also younger people that are just starting out as independent adults and have already accumulated regret. Journaling can help you with past regrets and it is important to deal with them now. The 5 simple steps will lead you to scripture that will set you free from past regrets. You will find love and forgiveness. This is so important because God wants us to have hope for our futures.

More importantly, as you develop your journaling practice you will find yourself making wise, informed choices. You will feel confident in your actions, words, and decisions. Once you discover this beauty, you will know that in one week, one year, five years, or at the end of your life, you will not be regretting your decisions.

Guilt can also take a hold of you and usually occurs in your current actions. For example, "I

Definition: **Regret;** *the feeling of being sorry, a sense of loss*

Guilt; *the state of having done wrong, to blame*

"'For I know the plans that I have for you,' declares the LORD, 'plans for welfare and not for calamity to give you a future and a hope."
Jeremiah 29:11

"Come now, let's settle this," says the LORD.
"Though your sins are like scarlet, I will make them as white as snow. Though they are red like crimson, I will make them as white as wool."
Isaiah 1:18

"As far as the east is from the west, So far has He removed our transgressions from us."
Psalm 103:12

---

am taking candy and feel guilty while I am doing it." Present tense vs. "Last year I regret I took candy." This is past tense. Journaling can help you deal with your current guilt so it will not find its way into your future.

Some of the hardest guilt can come from a loved one being ill, hospitalized, or in a care home. The guilt that follows—especially with a spouse—can be overwhelming.

- Guilt that you need time alone to renew your energy
- Guilt that you don't feel the same love for the person as when they were healthy
- Guilt that the spouse/parent/friend/child is sick instead of you
- Guilt that you can't afford better treatment/ accommodations/care
- Guilt that things were not talked about before
- And the list goes on

The pain is real. Journaling cannot take away the pain. Journaling will do two things for you.

Journaling can help you:

1. Work through your current feelings of guilt by embracing the moment, experiencing the pain, and bringing it to light.
2. Make wise decisions for the future.
a. Is there someone you need to talk to now?
b. Are your finances in order?
c. Is your support circle large enough? When people leave your circle through death, divorce, sickness, or moving, are you replenishing your support?
d. Have you forgiven?
e. Have you asked for forgiveness?

14

When my husband and I were planning a series of sessions focused on End of Life, I read a book titled With Purpose: Going from Success to Significance in Work and Life *by Ken Dychtwald Ph.D. and Daniel J. Kadlec. The book helped me to rethink the family unit. I am the youngest of seven children. My father was one of ten, and my mother was the oldest of eight siblings. I also have close to one hundred first cousins that are married and expanding the extended family. I came from a small farming community where my parents knew the parents and grandparents of my friends. I felt very confident in this immense network that I was raised in. There were ties and community connections everywhere.*

I now realize, being the youngest of my family, as my husband is, chances are my husband and I will outlive our siblings. I live in the city very removed from my childhood community, history, and roots. My family unit, due to distance and death, could dwindle to a very small number. I have one step-daughter who may or may not have children. We have no way of knowing how our life will unfold or where our support will come from.

Family members may not be replenished, especially with family units being on the trend of couples without children or with very few children. This is where friends and community can play a very important role. Friends can always be replenished if we reach out, and we need to work at developing this skill as we age.

Where is your support system and does it need to be replenished? Journaling a 'circle of support' diagram will help you to identify your current support system.

Circle of Support

Friends and family will come and go in your life due to location, interest, lifestyle, work, sickness, and death. You might know people who need or prefer more or less support than you do. This exercise is to get a snapshot of who the people in your life are and what type of support they will be able to provide to you in the future. You too will be a support for many people in your life through these relationships; however, the exercise is focused on who is supporting you either directly or indirectly. In order to live a regret and guilt-free life you will need encouragement along the way. Relationships that you develop throughout your life will help you achieve success, by reflecting what you need in your life.

Identify right now on this diagram who are the people, groups, and organizations that are involved in your life and write them down. There is a blank copy in **Appendix C** for future use, or go to www.sketchajournal.com to find additional resources.

Circle of Support Diagram

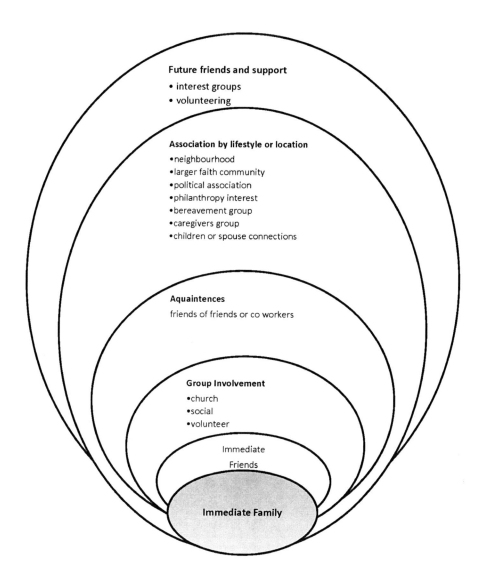

Future friends and support
- interest groups
- volunteering

Association by lifestyle or location
- neighbourhood
- larger faith community
- political association
- philanthropy interest
- bereavement group
- caregivers group
- children or spouse connections

Aquaintences

friends of friends or co workers

Group Involvement
- church
- social
- volunteer

Immediate

Friends

Immediate Family

Also identify who are the people, groups, and organizations that might be involved in your life in the future. (Maybe you don't have time or interest at this time but you might be involved in the future.) Take a look at your current and future support system. Is it balanced? Do you have a mix of ages, cultures, and lifestyles? Do you have people that can support you emotionally, physically, spiritually, socially, and intellectually? Do you have people that know your most personal thoughts and people you are associated with in relation to your interests or activities? If you see areas that are missing or unbalanced write them down on your diagram and start thinking about how you can add to your list. How will you meet new people if there are gaps in your support system?

Your life stage will influence your support system and it will always be changing. Who are the people that you will have a lifelong relationship with and who are the people that will come and go in your life? These are the people that will help you in your journey. Build your relationships to accentuate the positive relationships in your life. By building honest and trusting relationships you fulfill this need and help support people in your life. Use the circle of support diagram to ensure you are replenishing and sustaining your relationships. Journaling also brings clarity to your relationships and you will begin to see which relationships are healthy and which relationships are not healthy. You will be able to identity what you need to do to strengthen you relationships and how to build on values such as honesty and respect.

Relationships will be the reflection often needed to identify unresolved guilt or regret.

Let journaling take the current guilt from your life so you can move forward without regrets.

I received an item of inspiration when I first started the SketchaJournal Business. It read,

"Those who achieve success are those who take a dream and make it come true."

On first glance I felt encouraged and supported by my friend who gave it to me. I thought how great it is that my good friend is wishing me much support and encouragement for my business. I quickly imagined it being financially successful, influential, and recognized as a program with substance and quality. I could have carried on in my imagination some very grandiose ideas of success. What I did instead was to Journal about the word success. *I quickly realized that I wanted personal success before business success. I wanted to be successful in my relationships. I wanted to be authentic and I wanted to have a joy only my Creator would know how to fill. This would be what I strive for. I wanted all the personal success that I could be proud of so that at the end of my life (assuming I'm graced with a time of reflection) I would have no regrets.*

"And what do you benefit if you gain the whole world but lose your own soul?" Matthew 16:26

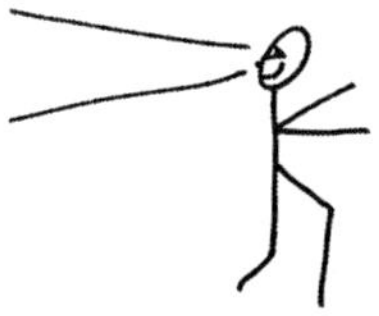

Figure 4
No Regrets

"In my desperation I prayed, and the LORD listened; he saved me from all my troubles." Psalm 34:6

What does success mean to you?

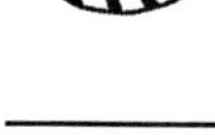

At the end of my life success would mean to me...

____

____

____

____

____

____

(Remember that the end of your life could be at any moment. Think long term and short term and see if they are consistent.)

Reason 5

How Focused Journaling Will Show You More of Life's Abundant Opportunities

"Know this well, then. (FIX in your heart) GOD is in Heaven above; GOD is on Earth below."
Deuteronomy 4:39

Figure 5
Focused

"But from there you will search again for the LORD your God. And if you search for him with all your heart and soul, you will find him."
Deuteronomy 4:29

"I can do all things through Him who strengthens me."
Philippians 4:13

When you start journaling you bring clarity to your current circumstances. You stop playing the endless mind games that can go on when you just think about your life, problems, goals, hopes, relationships, etc. Getting out of the web of your mind and writing on paper makes things real and you can start to separate reality from perception.

Journaling tools are used in the 5-step SJ Program to gain clarity and test your perceptions. Once you become vulnerable to God, God can reveal himself to you. Being concrete about your Christian journey will help you to identify and use the right journaling tools and scripture to maximize your prayer time. It will take some practice but once you develop the habit you will be amazed at the immediate results you will achieve. Instead of agonizing over decisions, words, and actions, you will be able to hone in on the root concern or lesson to be learned and move ahead with a focus that is solidly based on the movement of the Holy Spirit in your life.

Personal Note

When I was first starting my Christian walk one of the teachings was to focus on faith and scripture. Feelings come and

20

go and were not to be trusted was part of the teaching. I soon realized this was a very simplistic and incomplete analogy of using our intellects and hearts or our right and left brains. Emotions and feelings do change no doubt. We must use our wisdom together with our emotions to have a very balanced perspective when solving problems in life. By having our emotions and wisdom working together we sharpen our focus and have a clear intention of our goal.

Reason 6

Enjoy Flexibility that Suits Your Lifestyle

**Figure 6
Flexible in Time
and Style**

"God's various gifts are handed out everywhere; ... but they all originate in God's Spirit. Each person is given something to do that shows who God is: Everyone gets in on it, everyone benefits. All kinds of things are handed out by the Spirit, and to all kinds of people! The variety is wonderful."
1 Corinthians 12:4-7

Journaling is flexible in time, style, and outcome. The beauty of journaling is that it is so flexible that you can easily apply it and modify it to your unique personality and lifestyle. The tools, tips, and 5 simple steps that I will show you are a framework that you can put your own unique style on. How you will use it, is as limitless as your imagination.

Time:

If prayer time and reading scripture are already incorporated in your daily life then journaling is already a natural fit. The 5-step SJ Program includes scripture and takes it one step further. If you are already in prayer time it will not add more time; however, I believe it will be more effective. Journaling can be as simple as one word a day. Again, I say *simple* but it may not be *easy*. Use a few moments to really attune yourself with what happened during the day. Then think of one word that surfaces for you or captures the feeling or thought of the day. If you write one word a day for thirty days there will be a picture that emerges. It might be a theme that is repeated or a feeling that overtakes other feelings. By reflecting on your words you will have a good sense of your attitude and disposition. Are you pessimistic or optimistic? Are you thinking of yourself or others? You can Journal once a day, an hour a week, a day a month, or several days a year.

I have experienced the benefits of journaling daily and I hope you will also experience the benefits of journaling daily.

Remember, journaling is a tool to help your journey. Allow the Holy Spirit to direct you in how you will use this tool and how often.

Style:

I use the SketchaJournal because it facilitates the right and left brains to work together and complement each other. It forces me to think outside the box or out of my comfort zone. Hand writing is my preferred method for all the advantages listed below.

"Just as our bodies have many parts and each part has a special function, so it is with Christ's body. We are many parts of one body, and we all belong to each other. In his grace, God has given us different gifts for doing certain things well. So if God has given you the ability to prophesy, speak out with as much faith as God has given you."
Romans 12:4-6

• Slows your brain down, your thoughts go deeper • Preserves history, people tend to save hand-written documents more than typed documents or electronic files • Individualized • You can add more expression • Allows more flexibility and creativity • You can always find a pen and paper	• Fewer distractions than on a computer • Shows feelings • No distractions with spell check • You can sketch for added depth and understanding • Has the personal touch • More meaningful because it takes more time

Some people choose to Journal electronically and some people prefer only writing or only drawing. Any notebook will do; however, the SketchaJournal makes it handy to write and draw at the same time and will provide more creativity and flexibility.

Please copy the template of the SketchaJournal page in **Appendix B** or go to www.sketchajournal.com to print the template, which will facilitate the process.

Reason 7

Discover How Left and Right Brain Balance Can Maximize Your Life's Potential

Achieving Balance

How will you achieve balance in your life? Ask yourself this every time you are feeling unbalanced. I'm an avid believer that journaling is the fastest route to achieving balance. Journaling brings clarity, forces you to be authentic, and gets to the reality of your circumstances. When you think about concerns you can resolve some challenges. However, because you are a creature of habit you will find your thoughts swirling in your mind, thinking the same thoughts and trying repeated solutions that have not worked for you in the past. Until you change your routine thoughts, you will continue to recycle old information. Journaling and sketching force you to use both your right and left brains, optimizing your problem-solving skills.

Why don't we create balance for ourselves?

Balance in life is one of those things that people crave, want, and desire. We know it is good for us and we typically know how to achieve it. It is interesting how human beings behave. Balance can be the umbrella that oversees exercise, healthy relationships, eating healthy, and aspects of the environmental, spiritual, mental, and community life. There is enough information on the internet, books, radio, and TV. It is an information age. We know if we exercise every day we'll feel better. We know if we eat lots of vegetables and fruit we'll feel better; we know if we get adequate rest we will feel better. We know if we forgive difficult relationships we'll feel better. We know if we give, share, and help people we will feel better. Everyone wants to feel better; we know what to do

... however, we lack the inner drive to make that change. And the change can be minor and yet make a tremendous impact. It really makes you want to laugh at human nature. We have all become our own victims, repeating a negative tape of I can't, I can't, and I can't. Listening to Robert Kiyosaki's tape "Rich Dad Poor Dad," I grasped one of the most important lessons of creating balance. Ask yourself the question, "How can I?"

"How can I?" opens so many more doors because it engages your creative right brain. You will come up with fun, new, and exciting possibilities that don't present themselves when you say "I can't." Saying "I can't" engages your left brain that is logical, linear, and limited. Try to increase your creative ideas to bring balance to your life.

 Just for fun, write a goal or hope you have that will bring more balance to your life.

1) Goal

_____

_____

_____

_____

Now write all the crazy, unlikely, impossible, and possible ways you can achieve the goal.

2) I can achieve this goal by

_____

_____

_____

_____

God is full of miracles and wonders and you can tap into some amazing creative power: God in action.

How can you find what you need for balance ?

I believe strongly that you know what you need for your own life balance. You know what brings you joy, you know what commitments you have. You could not live a life of twenty-four-hour carefree joy, fun, and play without that voice in your head that reminds you that you need to put dishes away, wash clothes, review your banking, buy groceries, or attend to business. Likewise, if you are constantly working and attending to responsibilities then your *joie de vivre* will diminish and that longing for a vacation or time out will be constantly whispering in your ear. You are the best judge of what you need in your life and although you can read books on guidelines, they will never take into account all your nuances, personality, preferences, and life-giving activities. What is life-giving for an introvert can look so vastly different to an extrovert that they are not even speaking the same language anymore. The difference for you if you enjoy your job compared to someone who dislikes their job is so vastly different you can't even start to identify if it is balanced for another person. Only you know what feels balanced in your life. If you do not know if you are living a balanced life, your friends, family, or supervisor may give you hints. Take these hints and question them while you are praying and journaling. Ask yourself, "Am I spending too much time doing... or with? ..." With this insight you will begin to know what it feels like to be balanced. You will not hear any more *shoulds* in your mind. You will not be doing one thing and think you should

"And God confirmed the message by giving signs and wonders and various miracles and gifts of the Holy Spirit whenever he chose."
Hebrews 2:4

Who is this Creative Being we call God?

27

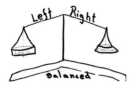

**Figure 7
Right/Left Brain
Balance**

*"Examine me, O
LORD, and try me;
Test my **mind** and
my **heart**."*
Psalm 26:2

be doing something else. Live in the present and check it out with friends, family, and coworkers.

As you Journal you will be able to answer this question as only you can for your life.

When unexpected events happen in your life it gives you a paradigm shift. This is what happened when my father had a stroke affecting his left brain and paralyzing his physical right side. A stroke of a loved one gives a 'very quick' lesson in how the brain functions and how the left and right brains differ.

Immediately I read and learned the different functions of the right and left brains and tried to understand my father with the perspective that his left brain was damaged and his strength would now be through his right-brain function. He focused on the big picture concepts; it was easier for him to relate to pictures and creative ideas than detailed linear thoughts and language.

We are fortunate that he has regained some of his language and can communicate verbally with us. My interest in the right and left brains was increased as I was taking a university course titled Creativity and Innovation and our teacher was handing out articles of contemporary writings about the left and right brains. It became clear that the current educational system focused on the left brain, leaving little opportunity to develop the creative right side of our brains.

I also began to think of my own style of prayer and how it skyrocketed when I started using images with my prayer journal, making the lessons powerful and lasting. It became clear that even before I learned about the left- and right-brain functions, I had already developed a more balanced approach to using my whole brain without consciously being taught.

I believe I was able to take this approach because of the numerous programs and opportunities I had outside of the traditional school system. At age sixteen I spent one year in Denmark and went to a Folkskolen. Although we had traditional classes, we were encouraged to be creative. I went from a very structured Canadian Home Economics class that taught us how to sew following a pattern exactly to a Home Economics class in Denmark that had us making our own pattern by measurements and creativity. It was liberating and freeing as I look back and recognize the use of the creative right brain. Having the traveling bug at seventeen, I then joined Canada World Youth, a program that focused on "Popular Education." This is where I learned the difference between Traditional Education and Popular Education. I learned culture, language, and how to adapt and be inclusive. Sandra Kerka, in her article titled "Popular Education: Adult Education for Social Change" (ERIC Digest No. 185), compiles a clear description of what popular education means. "... it is a form of adult education that encourages learners to examine their lives critically and take action to change social conditions. It is 'popular' in *the sense of being 'of the people.'" The process "Popular Education" uses is action/reflection/action or practice/theory/practice. I believe this process depicts how we can use our right and left brains to maximize our prayer lives. I would encourage you to read more of the article if it is of interest. Since my experience of "Popular Education" I craved a balance between my right and left brains, and have fluctuated back and forth from University classes to experiential learning.*

In **Section 2** of this book you will be able to practice the 5 steps, which lead you through reflection and action, reflection and action.

You will experience a revitalized prayer time by using your right and left brains together and begin to feel balance in your life.

Reason 8

Enjoy Heart and Mind Synchronicity

How do you use your heart and mind? Are they in sync, complementing each other and creating peace?

Have you ever felt that discomfort where your heart said one thing and your mind another?

Through journaling your emotions and reason start to work together, creating a balance and harmony between the two. They will work together in finding creative solutions instead of being opposed to each other. You sometimes hear people saying, "Well my head is saying one thing and my heart is saying another." This can cause confusion and stress and you might even start mistrusting yourself because you don't know which side of the brain is more valid—your right or left brain. I am saying that they are both valid and true, and the more practice you have working both areas together, the more unity you will find between the two. Your confidence will build because you will be able to say, "My heart and mind are in agreement."

You might often fluctuate from right and left brain to heart and mind. To me they are the same yet different. When you hear me say *mind* I am thinking of logic, reason, education,

"Then God will give you peace, a peace which is too wonderful to understand. That peace will keep your hearts and minds safe as you trust in Christ Jesus."
Philippians 4:7

**Figure 8
Heart and Mind
in Sync**

"Jesus said, 'Love the Lord your God with all your heart. Love him with all your soul, and love him with all your mind."
Matthew 22:37

"You must love the
Lord your God with
all your heart. Love
him with all your
soul. Love him with
all your power,
and love him with
all your mind. And
you must love your
neighbour as you
love yourself."
Luke 10:27

and wisdom. When I use *heart* I am thinking of emotions, feelings, intuition, but also authenticity. In the diagrams that show the left- and right-brain functions, you will not find the word *authenticity*, but I believe the right brain that holds emotions and intuition also holds your authentic self.

You might relate better to the image of your heart and your mind than describing your right and left brain. Scripture certainly makes use of the heart and mind where psychology might refer to the physiological aspect of the right- and left-brain functions. Please refer to the sketch in the introduction to review each aspect.

Reason 9

Living in the Moment Brings You Peace

Now that you have become more focused it is time to live in the present moment. You can only be responsible for your own actions in this moment of time. You may have heard the expression, "Yesterday is gone and we do not know what tomorrow will bring." The 5-step process is really about living in the present moment. Although healing from the past can take place and goals for the future are hoped for, each current thought, word, and action will bring you closer or further from God's intimacy in the moment.

"Where can I go from Your Spirit? Or where can I flee from Your presence? If I ascend to heaven, You are there."
Psalm 139:7-8a

Most of our world does not operate under a "live in the moment" mentality. People tend to live in the past or focus on the future. Why? I'm not sure. I guess if you have not dealt with the past pain, then it finds itself in your present thoughts and you can feel like it is happening now because you are reliving it. This is why I think the 12-step program for addictions has been so successful. They take the time to honestly look at the past, bring it to the light, try to amend any hurt or wrongdoing, and help others from their current circumstances and onward.

"Seek the Kingdom of God above all else, and live righteously, and he will give you everything you need."
Matthew 6:33

"And so I tell you, keep on asking, and you will receive what you ask for. Keep on seeking, and you will find. Keep on knocking, and the door will be opened to you."
Luke 11:9

The future is pushed on us continually through marketing, such as insurance and ad campaigns. The thought of, "I'll be happy when..." starts to infiltrate your thought process. We can be robbed of our happiness because we begin to think happiness is in the future and tomorrow never comes. Luke 11:9 says to "Seek the Lord while he can be found." This calls us to action now, in the moment. Don't wait for the 'what ifs' and the tomorrows.

Personal Note

I did a short exercise once and wrote about what would make me happy if I had time and money. My answers were simple, like pet our cat, write, read, Journal, and spend time with my husband, step-daughter, and friends. I'd enjoy music, dance, and food. I quickly realized that these were things I could consciously do starting that day. I did not need to wait for time, money, a successful business, or outside realities. In the beginning it was a bit like forcing myself to stop and pet the cat. But the more I did it, the more I enjoyed being in that present moment and the more I felt content and happy. People want to feel content and happy, and by bringing yourself to the present moment and doing things that are life-giving, you will be living this reality.

Things to laugh about:

I had missed my original Friday deadline to send the draft of this book in, so I was taking a Sunday morning to complete my edits and changes. I relocated my supplies and resource materials upstairs and was settling to start on this particular page titled "Journey in the moment." Our cat Storm followed me upstairs and rubbed up against the chair. As I learned to live in the present moment I also thought I'd rub her ear and she started purring. I thought, well, I can encourage her on my lap for a few moments if she would like. Storm was not really a lap cat and if she was going to sit on my lap it needed to be her decision. She jumped up and spent a few moments on my lap, then continued onto the desk and stretched herself completely

34

across my draft pages. I had to laugh because if I was to live in the moment I had to be with her at this time as she looked for more attention. I continued to laugh at my predicament and self-imposed deadlines and realized this is where Storm needed me to be—attentive to her presence in my life. The pen had to be put on hold. After five minutes she hopped back onto my lap, then relocated to a mattress for her nap. When I looked at my papers and saw this was a section about my cat I thought I must include our short encounter from this morning. One of the next books I will be writing will be called Everything I Learned I Learned From My Cat.

Some people self-sabotage their happy feelings or feelings of peace. In the core of our hearts and spirits and minds, we usually know what we need to feel nourished. We put excuses that are not a reality as road blocks. **I give some examples of this in Chapter 2.**

> Personal
> Note

I have learned many lessons from my husband since we met. Just to be in one's presence was an important lesson from our cat Storm, but I learned it from my husband first. Being the youngest of seven siblings on a farm meant for a busy life. The farm was pretty much self-sustaining, with growing our own vegetables for the entire year to having chickens, eggs, cows, and milk. What it also meant was it seemed like my parents were working all the time, except on Sunday when we went to church, ate together, played, and had visitors. My first few jobs were similar in that I lived and worked in the same environment and following a similar pattern of continuous work. The first day I met my husband he took the time to show me his workplace. I met him because I was going to volunteer there. I had been

---

Figure 9
Present Moment

a full-time student and busy with studies and exams, and it felt like I had no free time. When my husband took an hour of his day to talk, explain, and show me around, I was amazed. I thought, "Wow, how can a busy professional take uninterrupted time for me, a stranger?" This had not been my experience from moving from a busy farm to an even busier city. It made me pause and think, "This is nice not to be rushed around or feel that constant feeling of urgency." Later when I was starting my first company doing day trips for seniors, my husband came up with the name "Time 4 U Tours." My husband worked with seniors and often heard the phrase "No one has time for me; everyone is too busy. Even my children do not have time for me." By naming the company "Time 4 U Tours" we were saying, "Yes you are important. We have time for you."

I began to realize that as an adult it does not have to be all work. We need to add times of joy, fun, and renewal. Living in the present moment will help you feel renewed.

Step 1 of the 5-Step SJ Program is to meditate; by meditating you will be focusing on the present moment. The NOW! By journaling and identifying with the now, you can let go of past pain or regrets and let go of future concerns or worries.

Journaling in the present moment also allows you to take ownership of your actions and thoughts. You can't hide behind blame and frustration, pointing a finger at the world. No—this is about you, right now, and how you will use scripture and prayer to help you make wise choices.

I heard once that Psalm 46:10a is the first scripture that God uses to speak to our hearts, especially at the beginning of a conversion experience. If you think back on your own Christian Journey you may already relate to this scripture. I still find solace in this scripture above all other scriptures. When life is busy, difficult, or painful, and I stop and take a moment to reflect in God's presence, the result is that I am instantly reassured. Sometimes it helps to look at nature, such as a sunset, water, or the sky, to bring you to that moment of awe. In that very moment, that split instant, I know that everything is OK even in the midst of pain, confusion, or sadness. God is there in that moment.

Take a moment now to reflect on your breathing. Take deeper breaths and clear your mind. Imagine a busy bee stopping to sit on a flower. The bee has stopped being busy. Be in the moment.

Reason 10

Journaling Heals Your Past

"This means that anyone who belongs to Christ has become a new person. The old life is gone; a new life has begun!"
2 Corinthians 5:17

"When they had brought them outside, one said, "Escape for your life! Do not look behind you, and do not stay anywhere in the valley; escape to the mountains, or you will be swept away."
Genesis 19:17

It is difficult to live in the present or move forward in goals if you are caught in a tangled web from the past. Journaling will help you untangle the past and set you free.

Journaling tools can help you identify any unresolved pain, loss, and broken relationships by bringing the past to light.

You will be able to work through the pain by acknowledging it, embracing it, and letting go. It has served its purpose; now you can let it go.

Personal Note

When I was twenty-four I went to a Bible school that taught the 12-step program for a two-week session. At that point I was only familiar with the Serenity Prayer: "God grant me the serenity to accept the things I cannot change, the courage to change the things I can, and the wisdom to know the difference." As a teenager I had drawn hope, reassurance, and acceptance from the Serenity Prayer. As a young adult going through the 12-step program the presenter opened up what addictions might look like in our lives or, even more simply, said what has become 'unmanageable' in our lives. Using the

38

book Serenity, *a companion for 12-step recovery, all the students were able to identify with one or more of the addictive agents listed in the introduction. Once we were able to identify with a person or thing that we developed an excessive dependency on, we were then able to move through the 12-step program. Using the* Serenity *book we were able to cross-reference each step with supporting scripture. If you feel that you need extra support to heal your past I would highly recommend reading* Serenity *and beginning to work through the 12 steps that are clearly explained. Find a support group or companion that can journey with you through the process. By healing the past you will be able to live in the present.*

"So don't make judgments about anyone ahead of time—before the Lord returns. For he will bring our darkest secrets to light and will reveal our private motives. Then God will give to each one whatever praise is due."
1 Corinthians 4:5

Figure 10
Healing the Past

 Looking at your past can be your first step to healing. This exercise is meant to be very short and quick to help you get a sense of what you are holding onto from the past and what you have integrated into your life—or healed from. You can change the heading to suit your experiences. Take a maximum of five minutes to write down some key words that fit under each heading. Put a check mark beside those events that you feel you have healed from or that are not currently holding you back. Put a question mark beside the words or experiences that you feel you might need some support or healing from.

When you start the 5-Step SJ Program you might want to refer back to the question marks in the list and use it as a starting point for Step 1. See **Appendix D** for additional blank copies or go to www.sketchajournal.com to modify and print a copy.

Time Period	Relationships	Addictive Dependencies	Job related	Emotional Spiritual	Physical
Example Age 15-25	Gr. 11 bully √	Control? Perfection √	Pushed out of a job I enjoyed	Short bouts of Depression?	Did not feel athletic √

> **"Forgiveness does not change the past but it does enlarge the future."**
> **Paul Boese**

Reason 11

Creates Accountability that You Can Count On

To be authentic, whole, balanced, healed, and happy you need to be accountable to someone. It is often helpful to be accountable to a person, group, or organization. I challenge you to be accountable to yourself first. When we pause and Journal we begin to understand who we are, our motives, and our authentic selves. Who is more qualified than you to hold yourself accountable? Our human need to be accepted and liked often masks our limitations and sinfulness. We don't want people in our church to know if we have had an unloving thought or selfish moment. We don't want to disappoint others that might look up to us. This would also be true in your family relationships, organizations, and institutions. It is difficult to be vulnerable and still feel lovable, liked, and respected. By journaling, we can be vulnerable to God and ourselves. This is a safe environment. You can learn lessons through the movement of the Holy Spirit working in your life . God will challenge you to live a life worthy of His calling. By being accountable to yourself you will be taking full responsibility for your actions. You will feel empowered when you discover the secret that being accountable to yourself equals choices and outcomes. Jack Canfield, in his book *The Success Principles*, talks about the idea that events in our lives are not what influence our outcomes. It is

"To this end also we pray for you always, that our God will count you worthy of your calling, and fulfill every desire for goodness and the work of faith with power."
2 Thessalonians 1:11

41

our responses to an event that create our outcomes. By being accountable to yourself you will be able to choose your responses to events in your life and create an outcome worthy of your calling.

Reason 12

Journaling Propels You Forward and Higher in Your Ambitions

Once you are healed of the past it opens doors for your future.

Life is energy and it is important to keep it moving. Once you have cleared your thoughts, emotions, mind, and heart from the past it allows space for new opportunities, new thoughts, new emotions, and new relationships.

Journaling can provide a blueprint for actions and goals. This can be a conscious plan to achieve a goal, or you can allow each day to let the Spirit of God's Word move through you. It really depends on how you want to use journaling as a tool for your life. Once you have a routine or have developed the habit of journaling, you will find yourself looking forward to the moments of quiet time and insight. When you waver with a decision to Journal it can be time consuming and emotionally exhausting. This is the opposite of what you want. You want to be energized and emotionally alert and wise. Find the optimum time for you to Journal. Is it when you first wake up before you get busy with your day? Is it at lunch time when you need to step back and pay attention to how the first part of your day unfolded and readjust your thoughts and actions for the second half of your day? Or is

"No good thing does He withhold from those who walk uprightly."
Psalm 84:11b

Figure 11
Propels you forward

it at the end of your day when it's time to reflect and resolve any unfinished business? The time of the day is not important. It is the consistency that will produce the results. Things do come up, however, and you will need just a touch of flexibility to handle the flow of life as you commit time to Journal.

Journaling used with scripture in prayer will propel you forward in your faith and goals.

Reason 13

Love, What's All the Talk About?

Let me share with you a personal experience. When I was thirty-three my husband proposed to me. It was mid-June on the West Coast.

The day was warm and sunny and we had dinner at a restaurant overlooking the ocean. After dinner we walked on the beach where there were large logs that had settled on the sandy beaches. I felt so very blessed when my very good friend kneeled down and asked me if I would marry him. I had no indication that this would be the night that I would become engaged. However, earlier in the day during my prayer time I came across the scripture Matt 5:37.

"Let your Yes be Yes and your No be No." I knew that the earlier scripture was to be used at this time of being asked in marriage. I knew my yes was yes, and I had no doubt that God brought us together. I said a strong, bold yes with no wavering because I wanted my future husband to know that there was no doubt in my mind. The word yes was solid in my heart and I would not waver. In conversation that evening my fiancé, now husband, said, "Everything will be all right if we always

Definition: **Agape**; unconditional divine love or, as Plato used, to denote love of a spouse or family. **Philia**; an affection of brotherly or sisterly love.

"Just say a simple, 'Yes, I will,' or 'No, I won't.' Anything beyond this is from the evil one."
Matthew 5:37

"Where God's love is, there is no fear. God's perfect love takes away fear."
1 John 4:18a

"Dear friends, let us continue to love one another, for love comes from God. Anyone who loves is a child of God and knows God."
1 John 4:7

**Figure 12
Come from a
Place of Love**

*remember to come from a place of love."
I found it a bit peculiar at the time not
knowing the 'why' of the comment. The
words, however, seared themselves in my
heart and mind and I knew that a strong
foundation for our marriage had been set.
Journaling can be your foundation. It will
reveal to you when your actions, words,
and thoughts are coming from a place of
insecurity or from a place of love.*

Trust in the Process

Reason 14

Wisdom is Yours to Discover

How can you read and write about wisdom and not gain it? It is impossible. Scripture is full of wisdom and as you delve into the scripture and relate it to your own personal life you will find yourself wiser today than you were yesterday. It doesn't always need to be a new lesson or insight. It could be a week or a month that you discover the insight more fully with each day. Listen to subtle clues; you might come across other articles that support the lessons, or have experiences that reinforce the lesson. However it works in your life, it will be unique to you. The 5 steps are simply tools or a framework to start from. From there the movement of the Spirit will bring you on a journey.

Definition:
Wisdom;
1. Knowledge and good judgment based on experience, wise conduct, wise words

"Above all and before all, do this: Get Wisdom! Write this at the top of your list: Get Understanding!"
Proverbs 4:7

Reason 15

Effective Action Plans Will Guide You to Success

Figure 13
Build an Action Plan

You probably noticed that in business books you have read, or speakers that you have heard, they include a section on an action plan or writing down your goals. You will find this to be true in spiritual practices, business or personal self-help books, or talks. The thought behind writing is that it will be at the forefront of your mind; it is visual, it facilitates the 'Law of Attraction,' and it holds you accountable. What if you were to Journal an action plan to:

- Know God intimately
- Discover new ideas in scripture
- Be a more loving Christian
- Reach out to people and help

By journaling these ideas you gain perspective of the big picture. What do you want to say at the end of your life? Can you say, "I left this world a better place than when I came"?

With action plans it usually starts with a big picture or goal, and then you work backwards and break it down to small, manageable pieces or steps. By journaling the process you will be mindful of your goal because it is visual and concrete. It will hold you accountable and allow for the movement of the Spirit.

Reason 16

Journaling Helps You to Be Attentive to Nuances

Journaling is a great tool to find subtle nuances in your life. You will see opportunities where you did not see them before, which will contribute to your success in revitalizing your prayer life. Your prayer life will become more colourful and vibrant. You will see your life unfold in coloured pictures versus black and white. You will have a variety of shades of colour like what you would find in a paint store. Soon you will be able to string together a number of subtle differences that you felt were unrelated or disconnected before. Your journaling and prayer life will stimulate deeper conversations with the people you are in relationships with, as well as with strangers you may meet. You will start to trust in the movement of the Holy Spirit in all decisions and actions.

**Figure 14
Attentive to
Nuances**

You may have heard the expression "there are no coincidences only God incidents." When you start hearing and experiencing God's living word you will begin to notice God's message and the movement of the Holy Spirit in all aspects of your life. Your wonder will turn to wonderment as you begin to pick up messages and lessons from God throughout the day. God wants you to experience his love and creative spirit in music, friendships, nature, articles, and so much more. Journaling about your day and prayer life will help you to connect coincidences to God and you will know that God is in the midst of all those incidents.

Reason 17

Journaling Gives Insights and Wisdom

Definition: **Hone;** *a fine-grained whetstone on which to sharpen cutting tools.*

In practice: Zero in on, sharpen, work on, perfect

**Figure 15
Share Your
Insights**

Once you have developed the habit of sketching and journaling together, you will gain some tremendous insight into who you are, your values, hopes, struggles, and areas of growth. By honing in on these areas and understanding yourself you will be able to clearly share some of those aspects with your friends, family, and coworkers. It forces you to be honest with yourself, gain acceptance and understanding of yourself, and speak authentically to others without shame. If you have struggled at work with some tasks and are avoiding and trying to cover up your lack of ability, journaling will allow you to have the self-confidence to speak honestly. Journaling will allow some vulnerability into your life. Your working relationships will become deeper.

As a bonus, you will have a mind shift and slowly begin to understand other people by having heart-to-heart or authentic and honest conversations that go below the surface. Coworkers will begin to feel supported by you as you suspend judgment and develop an attitude of acceptance.

The 5-Step SJ Program starts with identifying issues in your current life and then brings you to a place where action is required. The action is to bring peace and balance in your life. By going through the steps you will gain insights into your motives and actions, as well as insights for your next steps. By changing your thoughts and behaviours you will develop a wisdom that is inspired by the Holy Spirit. When you share the benefits of journaling you are also as an offshoot sharing your personal journey with other people.

People will be encouraged by your story and sometimes it is just enough support to launch them on their own personal journey. Journaling will help you to articulate your story and it will help you to remember the process that took place.

Reason 18

Encourages Others to Journal and Live with Hope and Happiness

Figure 16
Be an Example

When you share the benefits of journaling with others they will be inspired. They will ask you questions and want to know more. When you plant the seed, you are allowing God to work through you. God will take the seed and provide everything that is needed over time to bring it to fruition.

Once people experience journaling with prayer time they will know the difference it is making in their lives. The movement of the Holy Spirit will guide the person through the 5-Step SJ Program and provide insights and wisdom.

Your role is to be a witness and example of the benefits of journaling. The Holy Spirit will do the rest. Scripture is the living word and, by using scripture in prayer time, God will be able to speak in your current circumstances.

Reason 19

Journaling Gives You a Snapshot of Your Life Review

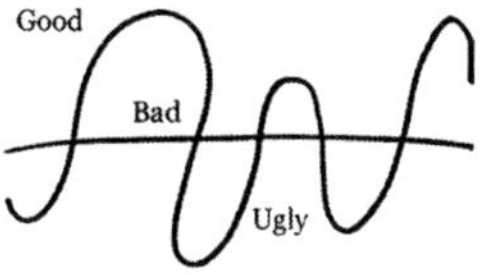

Have you ever found yourself on a Monday morning trying to remember what you did on the weekend? We easily forget our activities from the past and experience a mental block.

Figure 17
The Good, the Bad, and the Ugly

By journaling every day you can remind yourself of the lessons Jesus is teaching you. These lessons will become a part of you as you review and remind yourself of God's living word. Our minds can play tricks on us as far as the memory goes. If you are inclined to be pessimistic you might only remember the negative events of your past. Likewise, an eternal optimist might block out lessons from the past that were painful and only recall the positive points.

By journaling, you will be able to do a reality check to ensure your perspective is balanced.

Personal Note *In my workshops I ask people to look at the good, the bad, and the ugly. We need to embrace our lives to be authentic. We also need to look at the past to gain strength for our futures. You might tend to forget that you developed emotional or physical strength when you went through a difficult time in the past. These moments are important because you can quickly draw strength from your past and know that there are sunny days in your future. You will also notice that there were times in your life when life events were positive but you may not have felt positive. Likewise, there may have been some very difficult events in your life but you were not discouraged. Can you think of some examples in your life that your feelings were contradictory to your life events?*

Your Spiritual Journey will always fluctuate, going up and down, as will other areas of your life. By journaling every day you will have a clearer picture of what has been happening in your prayer life. Take the time monthly and yearly to review your SketchaJournal and discover what the big picture is revealing to you. When were your best prayer times and insights? What time of day was it and what season were you in? Were there unexpected joys or sorrows that changed your commitment, style of prayer time, or journaling time? By reviewing your SketchaJournal you can also pull out themes and ideas. What keeps reoccurring? Is it time to face some nagging issues and resolve them? Can you identify optimum prayer times and increase the circumstances that facilitated those moments? Does it relate to the time of day or amount of sleep? Were relationships positive during this time; were you being creative? Try to pinpoint as best you can what the triggers were that brought you down and what the things were that brought your mood up. Use your left and right brains to sort and compile the information.

What journaling will do for you is help you to be mindful of the lessons learned or insights. It will not be lost or forgotten. Use summaries so that you can easily scan your SketchaJournal and pick up lessons and insights that will help you in your future.

A Summary: A journaling tool where you can take time to review and reflect and then write down the key points. It will help you put the events in your life in perspective by looking at the big picture and integrating your past into your future.

"Reflection is one of the most underused yet powerful tools for success"
Richard Carlson

Reason 20

Find the Best Spiritual Companion Guaranteed

Who do you think your best spiritual companion might be? Is it your spouse, friend, religious leader, counsellor, or support group?

There are many people that God puts in our lives to encourage us on our Spiritual Journey. Some might be strangers or people that are passing through our lives. Others might be in a committed, long-term relationship with you, such as a spouse. Still, others might be what we consider to be experts in the spiritual, psychological, or emotional world.

Who has been with you since the beginning of your life? It is safe to say only you and God are always with you. You have seen your best times and your worst times. God had been with you each step of the way.

There were many times in my life where I looked for answers outside of myself. I wanted people to tell me who I was, what I was like, my gifts, and areas of growth. I wanted "easy to understand," "black and white" answers. It never gave me satisfaction, however, as comments always seemed incomplete. I knew I was different with every person I met and, depending on my mood, the day, or circumstances, my

disposition could look very different. This brings me back to the concept of living in the present moment. I know now that as I write I am living in the present moment and this very moment is the authentic me at this time. God is also with me in this moment.

When we listen to the silence of our hearts we can experience God's message to us. Our spiritual formation can go deep to our core being and prompt us to reach higher to God and God's people.

By being in tune with our feelings, realities, emotions, lifestyles, and relationships we develop strong foundations .

All the other teachings, support, information, advice, and counsel can be added to our foundations and build a framework. A prayer journal can be your spiritual companion that will unfold insight, wisdom, challenges, and hope.

"And I will ask the Father, and he will give you another Advocate, who will never leave you."
John 14:16

"When the Spirit of truth comes, he will guide you into all truth. He will not speak on his own but will tell you what he has heard."
John 16:13

Holy Spirit

Figure 18
Your Advocate
and Companion

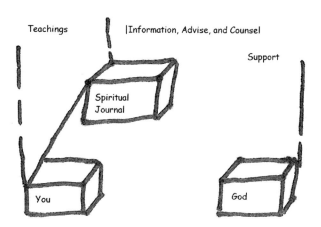

Teachings | Information, Advise, and Counsel

Support

Spiritual Journal

You

God

Reason 21

Journaling Creates a Stronger Relationship with Your Creator, Creating a Stronger You

"But the Holy Spirit produces this kind of fruit in our lives: love, joy, peace, patience, kindness, goodness, faithfulness, gentleness, and self-control."
Galations 5:22

"And I will strengthen them in the LORD, And in His name they will walk," declares the LORD."
Zechariah 10:12

"O LORD, my strength and my stronghold, And my refuge in the day of distress."
Jeremiah 16:19a

Journaling with scripture is like spending time with a best friend, reading intimate letters and discovering new things about you and your friend. Some books in the Bible are considered the love letters to you. Other books are like memoirs that share history. All the books together bring you different aspects of God your Creator , Jesus, and your advocate the Holy Spirit. It makes sense to say the more time you spend with scripture the stronger relationship you will have with God. Your relationship goes deeper and deeper. You understand new things and gain new perspective. It is not only about knowing God, it is also about you revealing yourself to God. It's about you being authentic, real, and vulnerable. You can take off the layers that hide your true self and start to shine. Your confidence builds because you know God is forgiving and loving. Scripture will present itself to you through Step 2 when you contemplate scripture. By having God reflect back to you, you will learn new and exciting things about yourself that you have not thought about before. You will discover that your self-confidence will increase, which will pave the way to you contributing positively in society. You will consciously choose activities that are more life-giving to you, which will benefit the groups or people that you are spending your time with.

"To be strengthened in your Inner self and to know the love of Christ that surpasses knowledge" Ephesians 3:16-21

By spending time and building your relationship with God you will be developing the fruits of the Holy Spirit. You will become confident and loving and carry the spirit of hope in all your words and actions. Your inner self will be strengthened and grounded in a way that surpasses knowledge.

"The Lord GOD is my strength, And He has made my feet like hinds' feet, And makes me walk on my high places." Habakkuk 3:19

Figure 19 Stronger Relationship = Stronger You

"To be strengthened with power through His Spirit and to know the love of Christ which surpasses knowledge." Ephesians 3:16b,19a

Chapter 2

Road Blocks, Setbacks, and Excuses to Journaling

Now that you have read 21 benefits to journaling you might begin to formulate some road blocks or excuses to journaling. You might feel you don't have the time, don't like sketching, or dislike writing. Maybe you have tried it before and did not find it beneficial, or maybe life got busy. I'm sure you could come up with over one hundred reasons why journaling is not for you.

Let me challenge you with two exercises.

 Exercise 1

Write down as many reasons you can think of on why you might not Journal.

For the top five road blocks that you come up with, I want you to Journal on how this could be turned into an opportunity.

For example:

Block #1 I don't have the time. I'm too busy.

Opportunity: Start with a positive statement even if you do not believe it at this time.

I love to Journal and I am so glad that I have the time to Journal because if I did not Journal then all my time would be filled with doing activities that don't necessarily bring joy, life, or change in my day. By journaling my time is more balanced with action and contemplation. I am a better person because I have stopped to be reflective. ...

Block #2 I don't like to sketch or I'm afraid I'm not good at it.

Opportunity: I love sketching because it reminds me of when I was young and I was not worried what other people thought of my drawing. I just drew because I liked it and it was creative. Sketching has renewed my excitement at being creative and I know that the sketching is for my own purpose to bring insight to my prayer life. By sketching I am using my right brain, which has long been denied the creative release. I know I can make circles. Add eyes and add expressions to my stick people. It is easy and fun.

Now add your own reasons and transform them to opportunities.

Block: I likely won't Journal because

Opportunity: I would love to Journal because

 Exercise 2

Ask yourself What am I getting out of not journaling?

Examples:

- If I don't Journal I will not need to be accountable to myself; that means I can let my morals and values slide on occasion.
- I do not want to be authentic because my facade has become comfortable and I don't want to be challenged.
- I don't want to heal the past because I have some good memories mixed in with the hurts and I want to keep my good memories.
- I'm not Christian enough or I'm currently sinning, therefore I think I should wait until I am a better person.
- If I become authentic, I think I will lose friends, lose income, or my status will change.

Now choose one of your examples and start a dialogue with God, Jesus, the Holy Spirit, or anyone else you might consider to be wise. Start with your statement and see how your wise confidant will respond. Then carry on the conversation for at least two or three pages. Your wise confidant might ask you questions such as:

"It is a trustworthy statement, deserving full acceptance, that Christ Jesus came into the world to save sinners, among whom I am foremost of all."
1 Timothy 1:15

- Is this really true?
- What else can you tell me?
- Is there more?
- What are you afraid of?

Me:

_____

_____

_____

_____

Dialogue Partner:

_____

_____

Me:

_____

_____

Continue the conversation and keep the pen flowing. Write quickly and do not analyse. See how the conversation brings you deeper to the truth and reality.

God knows what you can become. Start living the life you want.

Section 2

You will seek Me and find Me when you search for
Me with all your heart.
Jeremiah 29:13

I have told you these things so that you will be filled
with my joy. Yes, your joy will overflow!
John 15:11

Chapter 3

Intro to 5-Step SJ Program

You have read briefly about the 5-Step SJ Program in the beginning of the book and read 21 reasons why you must Journal for hope and happiness. The road blocks are really opportunities that you can use to motivate yourself and be creative.

I believe a successful program needs to be easy to understand, simple, and adaptable. The 5 steps you will read about also engage the right and left brains so you will find balance in your life. The steps all rhyme for easy retention: Meditate, Contemplate, Activate, Liberate, and Celebrate. I have included a definition and an 'In practice' explanation. The pictures are visual cues and there is scripture reference to support the concept. The explanations of the steps are brief and to the point, with an example to help illustrate each concept. The reason I chose to keep the steps very brief in explanation is because I believe you have the wisdom and knowledge within you. The 5 steps will help you to draw out the insights.

Journaling is very personal and active. All the suggestions in this book are to help motivate you and to get the ink flowing and the pencil sharpened. In this information world there is an overload of information and inputting into the mind. There comes a point where it is time to be creative and learn lessons and knowledge from within. By being creative you are engaging in life instead of being a passive viewer. You will notice the difference between watching TV for thirty minutes and journaling for thirty

1. **Meditate:**   What word is surfacing?
2. **Contemplate:** Find relevant scripture.
3. **Activate:**   Sketch the image of the scripture, and journal.
4. **Liberate:**   Decide what your next step will be and act on it.
5. **Celebrate:**   Thank God, and commit to an activity that renews you.

minutes. Try it and capture your feelings on paper to evaluate the effects of the two activities. Which one is more motivating and energizing? Which activity prompts you to be more loving, kind, and generous? With which activity do you feel more connected with God the Creator, family, and friends? We are made in the image and likeness of God and God wants us to co-create with him. So pull out your paints, colours, and imagination and see what kind of amazing life you can co-create with God. There is no limit to your imagination and creativity, so enjoy using them. There will be more inspiring thoughts that will flow your way. Ask questions like "How?" and "What if?" to increase your creative energy. There comes a time when you will need to put this book down, like reading about exercising or eating healthy, and get your body moving, or buying groceries. Now is the time to read briefly about the 5 steps and then start journaling.

Have paper, a pen, a Bible, and a concordance at your side so you can stop reading at any time and start writing and sketching. (A concordance is a fantastic resource book to be able to link your words to scriptures found in the Bible). Trust your heart and mind, guided by the Holy Spirit, to lead you on an amazing journey.

Now you can focus on learning, understanding, and experiencing the 5-Step SJ Program.

You will find the 5 steps and explanations on the bottom of each page to help you remember the 5 steps and what they represent. There is also a Quick Start Page in **Appendix A** called Quick Start: 5-Step SketchaJournal Program for the Christian Heart.

1. **Meditate**:   What word is surfacing?
2. **Contemplate**: Find relevant scripture.
3. **Activate**:   Sketch the image of the scripture, and journal.
4. **Liberate**:   Decide what your next step will be and act on it.
5. **Celebrate**:   Thank God, and commit to an activity that renews you.

This can be used as an easy reference or photocopied to share with others.

Once you understand the framework, then I encourage you to personalize the steps so they are meaningful for you.

---

1. **Meditate:**   What word is surfacing?
2. **Contemplate:** Find relevant scripture.
3. **Activate:**   Sketch the image of the scripture, and journal.
4. **Liberate:**   Decide what your next step will be and act on it.
5. **Celebrate:**   Thank God, and commit to an activity that renews you.

1. **Meditate:**   What word is surfacing?
2. **Contemplate:** Find relevant scripture.
3. **Activate:**   Sketch the image of the scripture, and journal.
4. **Liberate:**   Decide what your next step will be and act on it.
5. **Celebrate:**   Thank God, and commit to an activity that renews you.

Chapter 4

Step 1: Meditate – is Marvellous!

You will already have an impression or thought of what meditation means to you personally. I challenge you to broaden that definition just a little bit because in Step 1 it is not only quiet meditation—you will also put pen to paper.

Definition:
Meditate;
1. think quietly
2. think about, consider, plan, intend

Set the Stage

Step 1:

Find a quiet, uninterrupted space and set the stage to maximize your prayer time. You may want to light a candle, have a water fountain close by, maybe play some soft music (only if it enhances your prayer time), or have a plant or other item that brings you peace, a positive feeling, or a sense of nature.

In practice: Think and reflect, then write down 7-14 words that you were thinking about. Allow the Holy Spirit to bring one or two words to the surface and circle those words.

**Figure 20
Meditate**

Have your SketchaJournal™ for the Christian Heart or copy the template in **Appendix B**. Have some pens, pencils, and colouring items such as pencil crayons, felt markers, crayons, or watercolours. Alternatively you can cut out pictures from magazines and calendars to help with imagery. Have a concordance ready for **Step 2**.

---

1. **Meditate:** What word is surfacing?
2. **Contemplate:** Find relevant scripture.
3. **Activate:** Sketch the image of the scripture, and journal.
4. **Liberate:** Decide what your next step will be and act on it.
5. **Celebrate:** Thank God, and commit to an activity that renews you.

Make sure you are comfortable with the temperature or have a sweater that you can put on or take off. Take a few deep breaths and still your body and mind.

Meditate: Take a few minutes of quiet and focus on your breathing. Now, on your lined portion of the SketchaJournal, write the word *Meditate:* and quickly write seven to fourteen words that surface for you at this time. Write quickly without stopping so that you don't overanalyse this step. Often, words might relate to feelings, relationships, a concern, or a hope.

Concern: We had a business client that was not paying their bills.

Words that came up for me while I was thinking of this concern

Step 1a Meditate: Forgive, shrewd business woman, keep feelings in check, ask God's advice, trust in God, Trust, Trust ...

Review and Reflect

Now you are ready to look at the list of words you wrote down beside Meditation Step 1 and you are going to identify with one or, maximum, two words. Ask yourself, "What is surfacing for

1. **Meditate:**   What word is surfacing?
2. **Contemplate:** Find relevant scripture.
3. **Activate:**   Sketch the image of the scripture, and journal.
4. **Liberate:**   Decide what your next step will be and act on it.
5. **Celebrate:**   Thank God, and commit to an activity that renews you.

me right now? Are any words or feelings and issues repeated?" Is there a stir in your heart to focus on one particular word? Choose a word and trust in the process. God will lead you on a journey and give you insight. Be excited at the prospect that this is a word only for a starting point. You will be amazed at where it will bring you as you journey through Steps 2 through 5.

Feel the nudge. Listen for the still small voice

"And after the earthquake fire, but GOD wasn't in the fire; and after the fire a gentle and quiet whisper.."
1 Kings 19:12b

👀 **Di's example:**

Step 1.b. Choose and circle your word, i.e., (trust) came up three times. My word will be *trust*.

Optional Choice: Journaling is flexible and adaptable. What works for you during one prayer session might not fit at another time, or you might feel really stuck. An excellent alternative is during one session, take the time to write twenty-five to fifty words. Once you have completed your list (the more the better), you will prioritize the top seven words. What stands out for you the most? Which word causes the most stir in your heart, emotion, or conflict? Try to scan quickly through the words and write one to seven without overanalysing. One is your highest priority at this time. Begin to trust the movement of the Holy Spirit stirring in your heart.

---

1. **Meditate:**   What word is surfacing?
2. **Contemplate:** Find relevant scripture.
3. **Activate:**   Sketch the image of the scripture, and journal.
4. **Liberate:**   Decide what your next step will be and act on it.
5. **Celebrate:**   Thank God, and commit to an activity that renews you.

Once you have prioritized the seven top words you will look at the whole list again and try to group them in three to five categories (e.g., feelings, relationships, job, blessings, problems). Rewrite your list under the appropriate categories. Do you see patterns unfolding? Are there some categories that are much larger than other categories? Do some areas bring you joy and other categories bring you discomfort? Are your words seemingly more positive or negative? Lastly, remember the history log you wrote under Reason 10 Healing the Past? Look at the question marks and see what areas you might want to Journal and pray about.

These questions are just to stimulate some observations. The words, again, are a starting point to see where God wants to take you for the next 4 steps. You can use these words as a starting point for meditation on the days you feel stuck. Pick one of the seven priorities, or one of the headings/categories as a starting point.

There are many great resources from which you can learn more about meditation, in book stores and on the internet. You will find Christian meditation, Buddhist meditation, and variations of different meditations. For the purpose of revitalizing your prayer life, the simple procedure I shared above will be enough to move you through the next 4 steps.

1. **Meditate:** What word is surfacing?
2. **Contemplate:** Find relevant scripture.
3. **Activate:** Sketch the image of the scripture, and journal.
4. **Liberate:** Decide what your next step will be and act on it.
5. **Celebrate:** Thank God, and commit to an activity that renews you.

Chapter 5

Step 2: Contemplate – Your Call

Like meditation, you already have some ideas and experiences of what 'contemplate' means for you personally. Again, broaden that definition to include some quiet and active times.

Definition: Contemplate; look at for a long time, gaze at, consider thoughtfully, have in mind.

Step 2:

See if you can find scripture related to these words by using your concordance. It is important to have a concordance for this step of the 5 simple steps. You can buy a version for fewer than ten dollars or find a study Bible that already has one included. Now with the internet you can also search online for scripture. My concern is that once you are on the internet it will lead you away from a deeper prayer time and bring you to the surface or a shallow experience. You will need discipline to use the internet for only a few minutes or your attention will be whisked away to unrelated topics instead of going deeper into your spirit.

In practice: Find relevant scripture for your circled words and, contemplate the scripture associated to the word.

"When doubts filled my mind, your comfort gave me renewed hope and cheer."
Psalm 94:19

"The troubles of my heart are enlarged; Bring me out of my distresses."
Psalm 25:17

Quickly scan the scriptures related to the words. A concordance usually gives you five to eight words to get a sense of the scripture. Some of your words will have lots of reference

1. **Meditate:**   What word is surfacing?
2. **Contemplate:** Find relevant scripture.
3. **Activate:**   Sketch the image of the scripture, and journal.
4. **Liberate:**   Decide what your next step will be and act on it.
5. **Celebrate:**   Thank God, and commit to an activity that renews you.

**Figure 21
Contemplate**

scriptures and some might have very few. Choose one or two scripture and ponder the scripture, creating an image in your mind.

Step 2 - Contemplate

1.   What does this mean? Trust (opposite of fear)

2.   Sit with it and ponder. God Knows

3.   Find relevant scripture by looking up the word *trust* in a concordance. 2 Sam 22:3 Psalm 37:3

In some cases you might need to broaden a term; for instance, a sparrow or specific fish might need to be broadened to fish, bird, or animal.

Alternatively, if you can't find a word such as worry you could look for trouble or for happy, you would look for synonyms such as joy, encouragement, or hope. Select one or two scriptures that seem to be the best fit and read the verses and surrounding scriptures. Take a few quiet moments to 'chew the word.' Feel it, absorb the word, and listen for God's message to you during this time

Check it out and test it out. If the scripture absolutely does not fit then choose another scripture. You will be surprised, however, when a seemingly irrelevant or obscure scripture can

---

1. **Meditate:**   What word is surfacing?
2. **Contemplate:** Find relevant scripture.
3. **Activate:**   Sketch the image of the scripture, and journal.
4. **Liberate:**   Decide what your next step will be and act on it.
5. **Celebrate:**   Thank God, and commit to an activity that renews you.

come alive in the next 3 steps. Allow the movement of the Holy Spirit to lead the dance without questioning each step along the way.

> **"When you are inspired by some great purpose, some extraordinary project, all your thoughts break their bonds; your mind transcends limitations, your consciousness expands in every direction, and you find yourself in a new great and wonderful world. Dormant forces, faculties and talents become alive, and you discover yourself to be a greater person by far than you ever dreamed yourself to be."**
> **Patanjali**

---

1. **Meditate:**   What word is surfacing?
2. **Contemplate:** Find relevant scripture.
3. **Activate:**   Sketch the image of the scripture, and journal.
4. **Liberate:**   Decide what your next step will be and act on it.
5. **Celebrate:**   Thank God, and commit to an activity that renews you.

1. **Meditate:** What word is surfacing?
2. **Contemplate:** Find relevant scripture.
3. **Activate:** Sketch the image of the scripture, and journal.
4. **Liberate:** Decide what your next step will be and act on it.
5. **Celebrate:** Thank God, and commit to an activity that renews you.

Chapter 6

Step 3: Activate – Your Creativity

You have already been introduced to a number of journaling tools in **Section 1** of this book. You can use many of the tools during Step 3, the Activate portion of the 5 steps.

Definition: Activate; take an effective part in; participating; moving rather quickly, lively, brisk

This is where the dance truly begins and you maximize the use of your creative spirit and right-brain function.

In practice: Putting pen to paper, adding colour, using imagination and imagery

Enjoy

Step 3:

Figure 22 Activate

Rewrite the scripture on your sketch part of the SketchaJournal and engage your imagination by thinking of pictures, colours, and actions. Where do you fit into the scripture? Can you personalize it by writing your name and drawing yourself within the scripture? Engage your senses. What do you hear and smell, what do you feel? The idea of sketching is to have you co-create with the Holy Spirit in a unique and new experience that will revitalize your relationship with God by personalizing it. You learned how to create stick people and

1. **Meditate:**   What word is surfacing?
2. **Contemplate:** Find relevant scripture.
3. **Activate:**   Sketch the image of the scripture, and journal.
4. **Liberate:**   Decide what your next step will be and act on it.
5. **Celebrate:**   Thank God, and commit to an activity that renews you.

birds and the sun when you were young. You still have that ability to draw and sketch. Once you get over the notion that sketching needs to be perfect, you will set yourself free. The SketchaJournal is to be used as a workbook, not an art book. You want to quickly get thoughts and ideas and emotions out on paper so you can go deeper into your heart and spirit and hear God speaking to you, motivating you, encouraging you, and redirecting you when needed.

Creativity can be learned through exercises. Please see **Appendix E** for pages titled Expand your Creativity through warm up exercises

Draw nonstop and fill as much of the page as possible. Use words if you get stuck or want to identify with a picture. Add colour and exaggerate when possible. When God's heart is generous, then fill your whole page with one big heart; if you have scripture with joy then draw a happy face .

Simplified version:

Once your sketch page is filled with drawings, words, and colours, take a moment to reflect and see if you can pull out a one-line summary, insight, or message.

1. **Meditate:** What word is surfacing?
2. **Contemplate:** Find relevant scripture.
3. **Activate:** Sketch the image of the scripture, and journal.
4. **Liberate:** Decide what your next step will be and act on it.
5. **Celebrate:** Thank God, and commit to an activity that renews you.

Step 3 - Activate

̈ö̈ö Di's Example:

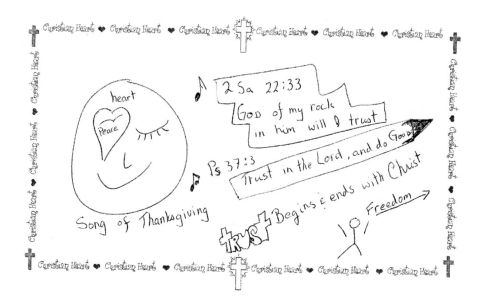

When I took the time to draw and meditate on the scripture from Step 2, 2Sam 22:3 and Psalm 37:3, I realized the word *trust* started and ended with the letter T. Right below the word *trust* I noticed the cross looked like the letter T. My insight was that the word trust begins and ends with the letter T, which looks like the cross, which represents Christ. "Trust begins and ends with Christ and I NEEDED to trust Jesus in this difficult circumstance."

Detailed Version:

A detailed version will require more time. It will also bring you deeper into a relationship with God. The detailed version uses

---

1. **Meditate:** What word is surfacing?
2. **Contemplate:** Find relevant scripture.
3. **Activate:** Sketch the image of the scripture, and journal.
4. **Liberate:** Decide what your next step will be and act on it.
5. **Celebrate:** Thank God, and commit to an activity that renews you.

more journaling tools that can either broaden your scope or hone it into a personalized message for you.

Three tools to try:

1. The Five Wise Questions:

This exercise is taken from Higher Awareness Journaling facilitation guide.

"WHY questions delve deeply into our main motives—why we do what we do. This process helps us go deeper in to our reasoning, habits and unconscious beliefs. This tool invites you to ask and answer a series of 5 WHY questions. For each answer that comes up, ask "Why?" to that answer. Do this process at least 5 times till you reach a deeper level of truth or essence."

2   Journaling nonstop for three pages

This is the basis of Julia Cameron's book *The Artist's Way*. The idea is to write continuously without stopping, editing, or analysing what you have written. Just keep writing nonstop for three pages or at least ten minutes. Once you are finished, then review what you have written, reflect, and write a summary.

3   Dialogue with scripture. Similar to Chapter 2 exercise 2.

This tool is particularly helpful if you really want to immerse yourself into scripture. Choose a character in the Bible verse to be you and have a dialogue with someone else in the Bible. Use your

---

1. **Meditate:**   What word is surfacing?
2. **Contemplate:** Find relevant scripture.
3. **Activate:**   Sketch the image of the scripture, and journal.
4. **Liberate:**   Decide what your next step will be and act on it.
5. **Celebrate:**   Thank God, and commit to an activity that renews you.

imagination and delve deeper into the scripture through your imagination. See where the Holy Spirit will take you.

At the end of your detailed journaling experience review, reflect, and write a summary statement, insight, or message.

---

1. **Meditate:**   What word is surfacing?
2. **Contemplate:** Find relevant scripture.
3. **Activate:**   Sketch the image of the scripture, and journal.
4. **Liberate:**   Decide what your next step will be and act on it.
5. **Celebrate:**   Thank God, and commit to an activity that renews you.

1. **Meditate:** What word is surfacing?
2. **Contemplate:** Find relevant scripture.
3. **Activate:** Sketch the image of the scripture, and journal.
4. **Liberate:** Decide what your next step will be and act on it.
5. **Celebrate:** Thank God, and commit to an activity that renews you.

Chapter 7

Step 4: Liberate – Your Heart and Mind

Once you gain a message or insight, it is time to put it into practice, or resolve a concern. Your prayer time has 2 more steps to go. Often, when we come to this point in our prayer time, we are:

1. Moved to have a change of heart or mind to be more Christ-like
2. Called to reconciliation in a relationship
3. Reassured of God's love for us

You need to liberate yourself from any negative ties and liberate the message or insight so it can carry a message of hope to you and the people around you. How do you do this? It might be obvious at this point that you are holding resentment or unforgiveness in your heart. You need to identify an action step to resolve this dilemma. You might choose in your heart to let it go or you might choose to speak to the person in love and honesty to bring about reconciliation. In either case you will be liberating yourself from negative ties and, as a result, you will be living in the present moment and one step closer to a regret-free life.

Definition:
Liberate; Set Free

In practice: Deal with current issues using prayer and scripture to heal. Choose an action that will bring hope and happiness to your prayer time.

"When doubts filled my mind, your comfort gave me renewed hope and cheer."
Psalm 94:19

"Make me know Your ways, O LORD; Teach me Your paths. Lead me in Your truth and teach me."
Psalm 25:4-5a

1. **Meditate:** What word is surfacing?
2. **Contemplate:** Find relevant scripture.
3. **Activate:** Sketch the image of the scripture, and journal.
4. **Liberate:** Decide what your next step will be and act on it.
5. **Celebrate:** Thank God, and commit to an activity that renews you.

Be doers of the Word

**Figure 23
Insight,
Learning, Follow
Through**

Worrying about a loved one is also emotionally and physically exhausting. Your loved one might have an illness, be at the end of their life, or be depressed. How can you liberate yourself from these very real and difficult times? God's scripture and your drawing will give you a hint and clue of what to do. God's message might be *Don't worry about tomorrow.*

"Seek the Kingdom of God above all else, and live righteously, and he will give you everything you need. So don't worry about tomorrow, for tomorrow will bring its own worries. Today's trouble is enough for today."
Matthew 6:33-34

Personal Note

I was in turmoil during a 5-step prayer session. It was over the Easter long weekend and I was feeling burdened by a difficult relationship. The scripture was Matt. 6:33. I realized for Step 4, Liberate, I needed to focus on the present and stop my mind from worrying about tomorrow.

In this case there might not be a physical action to do but you might use this step to hang on to the message of hope and know it and believe it.

Step 4 👀 **example**: Insight and follow through

- E.g., Who is my God? God is my God in whom I trust. Not $ nor clients, nor my husband to play the heavy. Must be respectful and as I write I use the pen of dignity. (Yes I am set free.)

1. **Meditate:** What word is surfacing?
2. **Contemplate:** Find relevant scripture.
3. **Activate:** Sketch the image of the scripture, and journal.
4. **Liberate:** Decide what your next step will be and act on it.
5. **Celebrate:** Thank God, and commit to an activity that renews you.

- Next step: Wrote out what I needed to say to the clients and then phoned to follow through.

Another way to liberate God's message and revitalize your prayer time is to share you insights with others. When you hear yourself speak, it reinforces what you believe and your experiences. The lessons go deeper into your heart and mind and have a longer influence on your life. It also will help other people understand you, as well as give you a new perspective or insight that could positively affect their lives or the lives of people around them. You will not know how far the insight or message will go, but it is a tiny seed being planted that God will take where it needs to go.

Commitment to Liberation.

Be sure to write down what your action will be and set a time frame. You want to live in the present moment as much as possible; therefore, procrastination on an action item will not liberate you or set you free. It is ideal to follow through with your Liberate step in the next half hour.

1. **Meditate:** What word is surfacing?
2. **Contemplate:** Find relevant scripture.
3. **Activate:** Sketch the image of the scripture, and journal.
4. **Liberate:** Decide what your next step will be and act on it.
5. **Celebrate:** Thank God, and commit to an activity that renews you.

1. **Meditate:**   What word is surfacing?
2. **Contemplate:** Find relevant scripture.
3. **Activate:**   Sketch the image of the scripture, and journal.
4. **Liberate:**   Decide what your next step will be and act on it.
5. **Celebrate:**   Thank God, and commit to an activity that renews you.

Chapter 8

Step 5: Celebrate – Your Life

I went to a course called Healing Soul Pain. The facilitators were trained by Dr. Jane Simington Ph.D. who researched pain and healing. Her observation is that pain lodges itself in the right brain (this is where the emotions are held). To heal from pain, grief, or trauma, it was recommended to do right-brain or creative activities. This would include music, dance, creative arts, drumming, and nature. I want you to be able to finish your prayer time in 'Celebration.' You have worked through the 4 steps and have gained wisdom and perspective. The prayer time may have stirred up different emotions or thoughts for you. You have liberated yourself and now it's time to Celebrate.

Begin Step 5 by thanking God for revealing himself to you during your prayer time.

Definition:
Celebrate;
1. Observe a special time or day with proper ceremonies or festivities
2. perform publicly, proclaim
3. Praise honour
4. Make a joyful time; make merry

In practice: Make a joyful noise make merry; What is life giving for you at this moment? Do it!

"In everything give thanks; for this is God's will for you in Christ Jesus."
1 Thessalonians 5:18

Thank God for inspiring your personal journey.

Write down a few sentences of gratitude for your prayer time and for the people and things

---

1. **Meditate:** What word is surfacing?
2. **Contemplate:** Find relevant scripture.
3. **Activate:** Sketch the image of the scripture, and journal.
4. **Liberate:** Decide what your next step will be and act on it.
5. **Celebrate:** Thank God, and commit to an activity that renews you.

"Then our mouth was filled with laughter And our tongue with joyful shouting; Then they said among the nations, The LORD has done great things for them. The LORD has done great things for us; We are glad."
Psalm 126:2-3

in your life. For example, friends, family, pets, food, home, job, sunshine, rain, etc. Lastly, think of a creative right-brain activity that you can do. Maybe spend five minutes dancing, listening to music, going for a walk, singing, drumming, drawing, taking a bath, or enjoying a speciality drink or foods—something that will take you out of the ordinary to the extraordinary.

Step 5. ◌̈◌̈

"For Your loving kindness is before my eyes, And I have walked in Your truth."
Psalm 26:3

Figure 24
Celebrate

- I.e., I felt free from guilt, I felt empowered as I was being authentic and honest.
- The effects are ongoing as the issue is reoccurring but my mind and heart have resolved the worry.
- 'Trust' was, is, and will be the answer.
- I chose to listen to Christian music to renew myself

1. **Meditate:** What word is surfacing?
2. **Contemplate:** Find relevant scripture.
3. **Activate:** Sketch the image of the scripture, and journal.
4. **Liberate:** Decide what your next step will be and act on it.
5. **Celebrate:** Thank God, and commit to an activity that renews you.

Call to Action

Journaling will change your life when you use it as a tool for hope and happiness. This is the call to action. You have read about the benefits, road blocks, and the 5-step process. There is flexibility in time commitment and style. If you have not tried the exercises in this book, I encourage you to go back and write a few notes. It is also helpful to have a friend that you can spend time with and work on the 5 steps together.

"The LORD is my strength and my shield; My heart trusts in Him, and I am helped; Therefore my heart exults, And with my song I shall thank Him."
Psalm 28:7

Start with a small sketch or a simplified version of the 5 steps until you experience for yourself the benefits. Once you have experienced renewed hope and happiness you will be on an amazing journey where surprises, miracles, and insights will be constantly present.

"These things I have spoken to you so that My joy may be in you, and that your joy may be made full."
John 15:11

Enjoy the Journey!

1. **Meditate:**   What word is surfacing?
2. **Contemplate:** Find relevant scripture.
3. **Activate:**   Sketch the image of the scripture, and journal.
4. **Liberate:**   Decide what your next step will be and act on it.
5. **Celebrate:**   Thank God, and commit to an activity that renews you.

Chapter 9

Conclusion

Mission Statement

My desire is that you live a beautiful life, directed by God, in a special unique way that is authentic for you so you can live life in the present moment and free of regret.

My personal life purpose is to be a Beautiful, Confident, Entrepreneurial Business Woman of and for God. When I wrote that statement I did not feel any of the words but I believed that was my purpose. This is what I strive for:

Beautiful:

I love beautiful things—artwork, sculptures, and flowers especially. I learnt for people to be beautiful; however, that beauty was from the inside. I was going through a period in which I did not feel very beautiful inside. I was managing staff at my workplace and felt I was critical, judgmental, and unloving. I did not like what I was becoming and knew that I had to regain beauty on the inside so I would feel confident and whole. Thus, I made the intention to take steps to be beautiful on the inside.

Confident:

I was having very low self-esteem and confidence and was spiralling downwards. I knew that I would have to find my confidence outside of myself because I had little to no confidence inside myself. From my relationship with God my confidence came from the outside in.

Happy:

Where had my happiness gone? I could not find it except for small glimpses here and there. I knew God would provide me with a "life full of hope."

Where there is despair Lord renew me and give me good cheer.

Entrepreneurial Business:

Over ten years ago I went to a career counsellor and identified that I wanted to be my own boss. I moved to the West Coast and studied Business Management in New Ventures and later started on my Bachelor of Business Administration in Entrepreneurial Leadership. I had ventured in one business doing day trips for seniors. I could not dedicate the time needed to create a thriving business without financial support and had to abandon the business to work full time. I went into full-time work but I knew at the core of my being I still wanted to be successful at my own business. I also wanted to be a philanthropist and knew a successful business was the only path for me to finance philanthropic endeavours. Teaching about journaling tools is my passion because I have experienced and seen the positive changes people feel when they stop and journal.

"She is clothed with strength and dignity, and she laughs without fear of the future. When she speaks, her words are wise, and she gives instructions with kindness."
Proverbs 31:25-26

Woman:

God's gift to me is that I am a woman. I cherish this gift and value this gift and embrace this gift.

Currently I am with child and feel wonder and awe at this blessing.

Of God:

I want the values of God. I want to experience and practice God's unconditional love. I want to know who I am, as well as what I am doing, is part of God's work.

For God:

For God is not only for God but also for God's people. All people are God's people. I desire to be inclusive, respectful, and loving.

Future Vision

At the time I wrote my life purpose I did not feel any of these qualities but the desire was so strong that I put it at the forefront of my mind. Through numerous journaling entries and times of reflection, my life began to unfold. It took some time before I crystallized my Entrepreneurial Business, but it is developing and unfolding. I believe this 5-Step SJ Program can launch your prayer life in a new direction, revitalize it, and impact the world in a positive and meaningful way.

I believe the system works. You just need time to reflect, which for most people slips away. You have a beautiful life that is unfolding. Take those small steps in the direction that you desire for your life. Find your Life Purpose and trust that you are on the right path. Receive from scripture strength and encouragement and encourage others as you go out into the world.

Send-Off (Scripture)

But you will receive power when the Holy Spirit comes upon you, and you will be my witnesses in Jerusalem, throughout Judea and Samaria, and to the ends of the earth.
Acts 1-8

Appendix A

Quick Start Page
5-Step SketchaJournal Program
for the Christian Heart
(with examples)

1. Meditate: What word is surfacing for you right now? (tired, worried, family, hope, aging, end of life, low energy)

2. Contemplate: What does this mean? Sit with it and ponder. Find relevant scripture with a concordance
   You can look for the word tired or the opposite which could be renew
   (Renew: 2 Corinthians 4:16 We are not discouraged rather, although our outer self is wasting away our inner self is being renewed day by day.)

3. Activate: Sketch the image of the scripture, and journal using your heart and mind to discover a message of hope and happiness in your life.

4. Liberate: Decide what your next step will be and act on it. (How can I take care of my body so it is not wasting away? I will have a glass of water a healthy snack and ensure I have a good night's rest for tonight.)

5. Celebrate: Thank God for inspiring your personal journey, and commit to an activity that renews you.
   (I will have 10 minutes of quiet time to be in the presence of God and write down 10 things I am grateful for.)

Appendix B

SketchaJournal Page Template

(Please see pages 98 and 99)

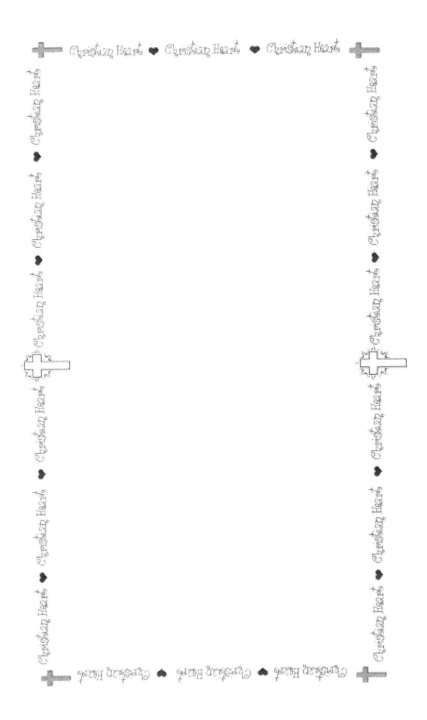

Appendix C

Circle of Support Diagram

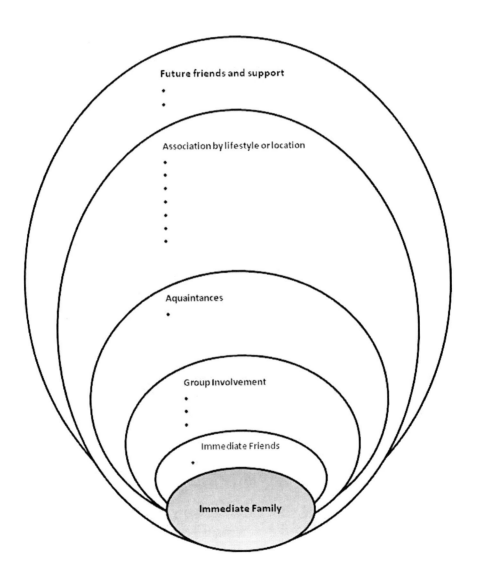

Future friends and support

Association by lifestyle or location

Aquaintances

Group Involvement

Immediate Friends

Immediate Family

Appendix D

Healing Your Past

Time Periods	Relationships	Addictive Dependencies	Job related	Emotional Spiritual	Physical
Example Age 15-25	Gr. 11 bully √	Control? Perfection √	Pushed out of a job I enjoyed	Short bouts of Depression?	Did not feel athletic √

You can change the heading to suit your experiences. Take a maximum of five minutes to write down some key words that fit under each heading. Put a check mark beside those events that you feel you have healed from or that are not currently holding you back. Put a question mark beside the words or experiences that you feel you might need some support or healing from.

Appendix E

Expand Your Creativity

Warm up exercises to sketch:

1. Draw circles: make circles the size of loonies and toonies or one inch in size
2. Draw faces: add eyes a nose and expressions to your circles
3. Draw stick people: with movement
4. Draw birds: make then simple like you did when you were five years old
5. Draw the sun/rain/ trees/hills/houses
6. Draw lines, spirals, zigzags, hearts, crosses, fish and more
7. Use crayons and shade a page with different colours and intensity
8. Clip out pictures from calendars or magazines

Warm up exercises to write:

1. Alpha Poem: think of a topic then quickly write one word for each letter from a to z
2. Write non stop for 3 pages
3. Start a dialogue and write for each character
4. Imaginary Now: Think of a date in the future such as one year from now. Start your journaling session by writing. "This was the best year of my life. Let me tell you why......." Be creative and write quickly two pages of your adventures in the last year.

Appendix F

Additional Resources

Retreats and seminars are offered to groups that would like to learn additional journaling tools for the 5-step program. Contact Diane C. Doyle at sketchajournal@shaw.ca or visit www.SketchaJournal.com for additional information and upcoming workshops.

Or write:

Diane C. Doyle
183 Pier Place, New Westminster, BC V3M 7A2 Canada

Current Workshops:

1) Journey through Transitions: Journaling on change, transition and grief
2) The Power of Journaling: An adventure in self-discovery and balance
3) Discover How SketchaJournaling Can Expand Your Creativity
4) Discover Your Life Purpose Through Journaling
5) Journey to the Christian Heart Through Journaling: in 5 Simple Steps

References

Cameron, Julia. *The Artist's Way: A Spiritual Path to Higher Creativity*. New York, NY: Penguin Putman Inc, 2002.

Canfield, Jack. *The Success Principles*. New York: HarperCollins Publisher, 2005.

Dychtwald, Ken and Daniel Kadlec. *With Purpose Going from Success to Significance in Work and Life*. New York, New York: Harper Collins Publishers, 2009.

Hemfelt, Dr. Robert and Dr. Richard Fowler. *Serenity a companion for twelve step recovery*. Nashville, Tennessee: Thomas Nelson, Inc, 1990.

Robson, John. *Go Deeper Reach Higher Journaling for Self Empowerment*. 2003.

About the Author

Diane C. Doyle: Developed the 5-Step SketchaJournal Program for the Christian Heart and created the SketchaJournal Notebooks.

Author, retreat leader, workshop facilitator, and keynote speaker, Diane developed and created the SketchaJournal notebooks to facilitate the process of SketchaJournal Workshops. The focus is on balancing the right- and left-brain function and bringing hope and happiness in your life.

Diane C. Doyle was raised on a farm in Saskatchewan and has since lived in Ontario, Alberta, and British Columbia. She currently lives in New Westminster, British Columbia with her husband, step-daughter Emma, and cat Storm.

An avid traveller starting at the age of 16, Diane has lived in Denmark and Costa Rica, and has travelled to over twenty-five other countries. Diane has found her passion in journaling and teaching retreats and workshops particularly focused on transitions and the Christian journey. SketchaJournal workshops help people through change and grief, or assist in journeying deeper to their Christian heart by going through the 5-Step SJ Program. Diane has journaled for over 30 years and believes journaling is the key to hope and happiness.

Photo by Claudette Carracedo

CPSIA information can be obtained at www.ICGtesting.com

226272LV00009B/140/P